What's the Big Idea?

39 Disruptive Proposals for a Better Society

Marty Nemko

ABOUT THE AUTHOR

Marty Nemko holds a Ph.D. from the University of California, Berkeley specializing in the evaluation of innovative programs and subsequently taught in Berkeley's graduate school. He wrote "The Big Idea" column for WashingtonPost.com and a column for TheAtlantic.com. He is in his 24th year hosting Work with Marty Nemko on KALW-FM, a National Public Radio affiliate in San Francisco. The archive of that program plus 1,000 of his published writings are free on www.martynemko.com.

DEDICATION

To those who consider my ideas, even if they end up discarding them.

CONTENTS

Reinventions of Relationships

Reinventions of Spirituality

WHY READ THIS BOOK?

Many people believe the American Empire is in its decline and fall. Indeed, a *New York Times*/CBS News poll[1] [1] finds that 39 percent of respondents believe "the current economic downturn is part of a long-term permanent decline." That is on the top of a CNN poll[2] that found that 48 percent of Americans believe another Great Depression is very or somewhat likely.

And Americans aren't confident that the proposed solutions will help much. A *Time* poll[3] finds that 62 percent of Americans think the U.S. is headed in the wrong direction.

Perhaps that's not surprising in light of the failure of the most recent round of remedies: Despite massive corporate bailouts, government stimulus spending, and massive quantitative easing, the economy remains precarious-- Do people you know say it's easy to find a good job? .

And education, the supposed magic pill, has been more of a placebo. For decades now, the U.S. has ranked #1 or 2 in per-capita education spending yet continues to lag in the most recent international comparison[4], tied for 23rd with Poland, while Shanghai, China, which spends far less per capita on education, ranks #1.

Ironically, such solutions are inadequate in part because we're a democracy. Policies are adopted only after being embraced by a diverse array of experts, the public, legislators, and political leaders. While that approach ensures broad buy-in, it tends to create tepid, relatively impotent policy--that on which nearly everyone can agree, a lowest common denominator. Policies that offend no one, that step on no one's toes, are unlikely to produce major improvements.

It is time to at least consider bolder solutions, those not shackled by the need to obtain consensus. This book's proposals are disruptive, solutions that hold greater promise than do more universally comfortable policies. This book offers a blueprint for reinventing 39 of society's pillars.

[1] *The endnotes are for readers of the print version of this book. They provide the web address for each link.*

I believe in crowd-sourcing, so at the end of each *reinvention*, I include a link to its page on my blog, so you can comment. I'll incorporate your input and discuss the resulting reinventions with the highest-level policymakers I can access.

I want to be respectful of your time. So this book will be as brief as possible, presenting only each reinvention's essential elements.

And in that spirit of brevity, enough introduction. On to the reinventions.

1
HOW WE THINK, REINVENTED

As individuals and as a country, we make many bad decisions because we haven't paid enough attention to cost/benefit. Examples:

Anti-Terrorism

Requiring all airline passengers to take off their shoes has a near-zero chance of stopping a terrorist attack. Terrorists know that all shoes are screened so, of course, they'll put a bomb, for example, in a body cavity. Or they'll use an almost impossible-to-stop attack: open a vial of communicable biovirus in the pre-screening lobby of an international terminal, its parking lot shuttle, or in a sports arena. Or inject it in fruit in a supermarket or into a suburb's not-very-secure water reservoir. Or detonate a suitcase nuke in a car trunk in a busy downtown.

The shoe removal/re-donning ritual on top of other low-payoff, time-consuming airport screens such as double-inspecting your boarding pass and ensuring that your toothpaste weighs less than three ounces, wastes countless hours of passengers' time and a fortune of our tax dollars in airport security personnel.

In addition, lengthening security screening decreases demand for air travel[5], which hurts the struggling airlines and all employers that otherwise would have chosen an in-person meeting over a tele- or videoconference.

And more personally, it means that grandparents less often get to see grandkids, long-distance lovers to see sweetie.

Our policymakers need to make decisions more on cost-benefit.

Investing

Seventy-seven percent of mutual fund buyers choose actively managed mutual funds rather than index funds[6] and exchange-traded funds, even though decades of data are clear that index investors do better[7].

Faith in God

A Google search on "Surrender to God" yields 900,000 results. Millions of people follow the Bible's urging to be passive, to wait for God to provide. For example,

> Philippians 4:19 Be not wise in your own eyes; God shall supply all your need.

> Proverbs 3:1: Trust in the Lord with all your heart, and do not lean on your own understanding.

> 1 Corinthians 10:17 God is faithful, and he will not let you be tempted beyond your ability,

> Matthew 17:20 If you have faith like a grain of mustard seed, you will say to this mountain, 'Move from here to there,' and it will move, and nothing will be impossible for you.

What are the odds there is an omniscient, omnipotent deity watching the seven billion people's every move to ensure they all do okay? Forget about whether such advice will result in your landing a good job in this economy. Remember that billions of people, including newborns have died screaming in agony. And what about all those catastrophic earthquakes and epidemics? And **if "God will provide," why do billions of the world's people lack basic food, water, shelter, and health care?** Could anyone who makes decisions based on cost/benefit "surrender to God?"

Attempting to Close the Achievement Gap

We continue to bet endless billions of dollars on education as the tool most likely to close the achievement gap. That, despite more than a half-century and trillions of dollars[8] (also see this[9]) spent trying so many permutations and combinations of teaching style, curriculum, etc., Yet the achievement gap remains as wide as ever[10]. We haven't been able to do better than to tout a non-replicable superstar teacher or pilot program: from Marva Collins (her school is now closed due to lack of enrollment[11]) to Michelle Rhee's DC non-miracle[12], to bad-data KIPP[13], to the latest fad, Khan Academy. Go take a Khan Academy lesson[14] and ask yourself if a year of that is likely to close the algebra achievement gap. They're boring[15]. Only highly motivated students will learn algebra that way. Do you really think America's low achievers will learn algebra so much better with Khan lessons as to close the achievement gap?

Yet we continue to prefer to bury our heads in the sand and bet a fortune and our children's future that the next classroom innovation du jour will close the achievement gap. Is it not time to start thinking cost-benefit: Could the enormous costs of those classroom programs, trainings, etc., be more wisely spent? For example, mightn't it be wise to accept that we aren't close to figuring out how to close the achievement gap and so rather than spending more trillions on unlikely-to-work classroom programs, reallocate those dollars to fundamental research aimed at figuring out the foundational roots of the achievement gap, and only then to develop programs based on those roots, and if there's money left, to return it to the taxpayer?

A Solution

The most important thing schools and colleges should teach is how to think rationally: cost/benefit, risk/reward, opportunity costs. But we're too busy teaching the periodic table of elements, the causes of the War of 1812, the intricacies of Shakespeare, and how to solve quadratic equations.

To comment, click HERE[16].

REINVENTIONS OF NATIONAL POLICY

2
HOW WE SELECT OUR LEADERS, REINVENTED

More and more money pours into election campaigns, heavily from special interests. That enables ever-more sophisticated Madison-Avenue types to spend a fortune on truth-obfuscating messaging to manipulate us. Today, nearly every sentence spoken by major politicians is dial focus-group tested.

As troubling, those special interests wouldn't be pouring billions into campaigns unless they were confident it would result in politicians doing their bidding rather than what's best for us all. The following would ensure we elect better and less-corrupted leaders:

- All campaigns would be 100% publicly-funded. This has been proposed and rejected in the past as a denial of free speech. I believe that abridgment is far outweighed by the benefit to society.

- All campaigns would be just two weeks long. That would control cost and only minimally reduce voter knowledge: Most voters have long forgotten what they heard earlier about the candidates.

- The campaigns would consist only of one or two broadcast debates. Those would be followed by a job simulation: running a meeting.

- A neutral body such as C-Span or Consumers Union would post each major candidate's biographical highlights, voting record, and platform on key issues.

Such a system would reduce candidates' corruptibility while increasing the quality of information voters would have about the candidates. As important, better candidates would run, knowing they needn't run an endless, expensive, press-the-flesh, beholden-to-special-interests campaign.

An even more different approach

Our government officials would be selected, not by voting, but using passive criteria. For example, the Senate might consist of the most newly retired of the 10 largest nonprofits, a randomly selected CEO of the S&P Midcap 400, the Police Officer of America's Cop of the Year, the National Teacher of the Year, the most award-winning scientist under age 30, etc., plus random citizens.

The benefits of this system include:

— We'd have a more worthy and ideationally diverse group of leaders.

— Because there would be no campaigns, our leaders would not be beholden to big donors.

— The public would view such a leadership with more respect than they have for our elected candidates.

— The absence of campaigns would save the public a fortune. Just our income tax form's $3-per-person check-off box to political campaigns is projected to, over the next 10 years, cost the taxpayer $617 million[17].

Of course, one might argue that the incumbent politicians would never allow it. After all, the foxes are guarding the hen house. But I believe the media, equally eager to see better leaders, would urge the electorate to support candidates who would vote for a fairer selection system. And politicians, concerned about their place in history, will feel pressure to support the change. History would view politicians that voted themselves out of a job for the good of the nation as heroes, while no-voting politicians would be seen as self-serving obstructionists.

Another objection is that a "Don't Elect. Select."-program would require a Constitutional amendment, which is no easy task, but the Constitution has already been amended 27 times. I can't think of a more worthy reason for number 28.

To comment, click HERE[18].

3
OUR APPROACH TO MEN, REINVENTED

I appreciate the women's movement. For example, it may have helped my daughter become Assistant U.S. Attorney and my wife become Napa County Superintendent of Schools.

And I've certainly heard that women deserve more, for example, "It's still a man's world. After all, most CEOs and all the presidents are men, and women overall earn 77 cents on the dollar."

But I invite you to consider a different perspective.

Let me start by inviting you to imagine a world without men. You wouldn't be able to read this: no computer, no computer screen. Probably no chair you're sitting on, no air conditioner/heater that's making you comfortable in your room. For that matter, you wouldn't have a room--It and its materials were likely developed and installed by men: from the sub-floor to the roof. So are the birth control pill that kept you from getting pregnant, the refrigerator that kept your baby's formula and your food fresh, the car that gives you freedom of movement or the mass transit that environmentalists prefer. Beyond necessities, men have given us information transmitters from the printing press to the television to Google to the iPhone, wisdom from Plato and Plutarch to Kant and Kafka, Victor Davis Hanson to Christopher Hitchens, and presidents from George Washington to Barack Obama. And lest all work and no play make dull boys and girls, men have given us entertainment from Shakespeare to Spielberg, Rembrandt to Rothko, Beethoven to Basie to the Beatles to Bono. You might not even be able to defecate without men: What percentage of toilets would you guess were built, installed, and repaired, not to mention sewer lines cleaned out, by women? No less than lesbian feminist, Camille Paglia wrote, "If civilization had been left in female hands, we would still be living in grass huts.[19] "

Bad times for men

Yet over the past half century, as a side effect of the appropriate increase in women's opportunities, there has been an accelerating effort, a successful effort, to diminish men. Just a couple of obvious manifestations: President Clinton's Press Secretary Dede Myers', book "Why Women Should Rule the World" and *New York Times* columnist Maureen Dowd's bestseller, "Are Men Necessary?"

Even more telling is Hanna Rosin's cover story of a Father's Day edition of *The Atlantic*. Its title: 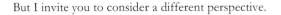*The End of Men.*[20] Its core contention is that men are better suited for the Neanderthal Era and Industrial Revolution, when success usually depended on brawn and individual testosterone-"poisoned" competition. Rosin argues that today's success requires women to be in charge. She writes, for example, "Men are women's new ball and chain," and "Maybe...(male) DNA is shifting. Maybe they're like those frogs--they're more vulnerable or something, so they've gotten deformed."

Yet somehow, men have accomplished the aforementioned.

The male-bashing dispirits not only the intellectual men who read publications such as *The Atlantic*. Average men and boys are force-fed a diet ever-more larded with images of boorish, sleazy, idiotic men shown the way by wise women. We're in our seventh decade of man-as-oaf media: from Ralph Kramden to Homer Simpson. Even in the majority-male Superbowl audience, commercials constantly present man as cretin: hopelessly impotent men who are literally in the doghouse, cowed by their woman[21] master. Or they're mumbling supplicants begging for a woman judge's charity. Lest you think I'm cherry-picking, turn on your TV: How often does a show or commercial portray the man as superior to a woman?

Twenty-five years ago, when I began helping people choose their career, both sexes were equally optimistic about their future. Today, except at the C-level, at which fewer women are willing to work the 60+-hour weeks, take the years to get technical enough, and to move their families across the country to get the necessary promotions, most of my female clients correctly believe the world is their oyster. And my male clients are disproportionately despondent and/or angry...

And not going to college. In 1960: the male/female ratio of college degree holders was 61/39. Today, in an era in which a college degree has become a virtual necessity, a mere hunting license for most decent employment, the ratio has completely reversed: It's 60/40 in favor of women[22]. Yet despite men's serious underrepresentation, many scholarships are set aside for women, few for men. Student groups are funded to encourage women, for example, future businesswoman groups, far fewer for men.

So it's not surprising that men's unemployment rate[23] is now higher than women's. As you know, so many young men are back living with their parents, drunk, stoned and/or playing video games while the young women are launching their career.

"Women earn 77 cents on the dollar!" A misleading statistic

But what about the much-trumpeted statistic that women earn just 77 cents for every dollar men earn? The statistic implies that, *for the same work*, women are paid less. The evidence indicates that far more often, there are *fair* reasons why men are paid more. For example, among people claiming to work full time, men work an average of six hours a week longer and work more continuous years and so are paid more. Ninety-two percent of workplace deaths[24] and severe workplace injuries (e.g., amputations, black lung disease) occur to men, so they get paid more for choosing dangerous work.

15

Special note need be made of the military: 97.5 percent of the deaths in the Iraq and Afghanistan wars have been men[25]. Perhaps that's surprising in light of the media's hiding that with such phrases as "the men and women serving in Afghanistan." One might ask, why are only men allowed to serve in direct combat? Why are only men required to register for the draft?

Even within a profession, when men earn more, there are reasons other than sexism. For example, male physicians earn more but that's because they are more likely to choose specialties such as surgery or cardiology which are higher-stress, have more irregular hours, and require longer residencies, while women are more likely to choose pediatrics or general practice.

A rich research literature documents that sexism is not at the core of pay differentials, for example, THIS[26] is from the *New York Times, THIS[27] is from the Wall Street Journal, THIS[28] is from Compensation Cafe, THIS[29] is from City Journal.* Alas, the media chooses to ignore all that research in favor of the broad-brush, "Women earn 77 cents on the dollar."

Today's unfair policies and practices

Rather than trying to help men close their unemployment gap, the government deliberately exacerbates men's deficit. For example, government pressures businesses to have "targets," virtual quotas, for women (a "protected class,"), but not for men. And women-owned businesses receive special preferences in landing government contracts, for example, THIS[30].

Corporations themselves deliberately exacerbate the unfairness to men. Women but not men are encouraged to form committees and caucuses to advance their sex in the workplace, often at men's expense. Examples: mentor programs for women only, special training for women only, fast-track-to-executive position for women only

Rather than demand work-life balance, men are more likely than women to throw all of themselves into work, for which they are often dubbed with such pathologizing monikers as "workaholic", "out of balance," and "unable to relax" rather than "heroic" for being so contributory, even if it costs them their life. Indeed, men die 5.2 years earlier than women[31], a major cause being stress-related illnesses such as heart attack and stroke.

True, the occasional foolish old boy still unfairly promotes a man over a woman but despite unemployment being higher for men than women, today, "Sisters help Sisters" is not denigrated let alone sued as sexist, but encouraged. For example, former U.N. Ambassador Madeleine Albright said, "There is a special place in hell for women who don't help other women[32]." And such statements have broad impact. For example, a Google search on that sentences reveals 98,800 matches.

Men's efforts to organize into groups have typically been ridiculed, for example, portraying men's groups as troglodytes tromping into the woods to beat tom-toms. And men's organizations have been pressured to admit women, for example, the service clubs: Rotary, Kiwanis, and Lions, while the long-female-only Soroptomists[33] remains that way. Further limiting men's ability to organize, men's groups don't get the enormous free advertising the media gives to women's groups.

Serious unfairnesses to men extend much further. Examples: In an era of higher unemployment for men than women, why do men still more often pay for dates? Why do women, more often than men, feel okay about dumping their spouse or boyfriend because he doesn't make enough money? Is it fair that if a man makes the momentary error of impregnating a woman, even if she falsely claimed to be on birth control, he's stuck with 18 years of financial and parenting responsibility? Is it fair that only the woman has the choice to abort a child? Is it fair that the EEOC's new definition of rape includes this: If you've had one drink, then had sex and later claim it was unwanted, it's rape[34].

And what about men who need social services? Countless social services focus on women, far fewer on men, even though, for example, men's suicide rate is four times as high. [35]

And in the worst unfairness to men, when women have a deficit, for example, they're "underrepresented" in science, we see massive redress despite the two-decade study reported in the *New York Times* that found that women in academic science fare as well or better than men[36]. Yet when men have the ultimate deficit--as mentioned, they live 5.2 years shorter--a search of PubMed, which indexes 3,000 medical journals for the last 60 years, on the terms "women's health" and men's health," reveals 43 times(!) as many studies using "women's health." And in terms of outreach, there's a sea of pink ribbons but only a trickle for prostate cancer and even less for sudden heart attack, which kills many more men and earlier. There are seven federal agencies on women's health, none for men. 39 states have offices of Women's Health, none for men. Bottom line: Since 1920, the average lifespan advantage of women **has grown 400%[37]!**

Some feminists shrug that off with such statements as, "Well, women were previously excluded from those studies. They didn't care about women." In fact, when women were underrepresented in studies, it was usually because:

- Fewer women volunteer for the risk of experimental treatment
- Fewer women are in prison, a major source of subjects.
- Researchers appropriately did not want to risk exposing women of childbearing age to an experimental drug that could damage a fetus.

Other feminists blame men's dying younger on their not taking as good care of themselves: "If only they'd see the doctor." Well, would those feminists say that to

African-Americans, who also "don't see the doctor" and smoke and drink at higher rates than men?

Alas, things will likely get even worse for the next generation of men. Have you not seen "Girls Rule[38]" tee shirts? How do you think that makes boys feel? More seriously, the U.S. school system has heavily replaced boy-friendly competition with girl-centric collaboration, boy-friendly adventure stories, with soporific-to-boys tales of girl relationships, and created new history textbooks disproportionately extolling women from Sacajawea and Pocahontas to Simone DeBouvier and Sally Ride while sparing no pages to pound home the evils of white men from Hannibal to Hitler, Joe McCarthy to Timothy McVeigh. And when children can't endure school's large amount of seatwork, boys are put on a Ritalin leash at a ratio of eight boys for every one girl.

While, of course, one can point to examples of unfairness to women, it's wrong to assert that today, men, on balance, have an unfair advantage.

A plan for fairness to both sexes

The world is better when both sexes are valued. For every customer-cheating, wife-beating, sexual harassing guy, there's at least one ethical man, working hard to be productive and to support himself and his family. For every manipulative, hormonally crazed, girls-just-want-to-have-fun woman, there's at least one woman diligently striving to have it all: career, family, and a personal life. Good people all. People with real potential to make a better society for all.

It's time for a truce, one that's fair to both sexes:

1. We must end the gender-bashing, male or female, in the schools, colleges, and media.

2. It's time to end intentional discrimination against both women and men, as documented in the examples above.

3. To the extent that men could use better communication skills and more collaborative leadership styles to accompany the more goal-oriented individualistic ones, instead of dismissing such men as unable to communicate, let our schools, colleges, and workplaces offer such trainings.

4. It's time for serious Men's Studies programs at universities that don't merely parrot the unfairly male-bashing rhetoric of women's studies.

5. It's time to pay due homage to men, who do so many of the dangerous jobs women won't do (from roofer to rodent remover,) and invent the aforementioned things that women hadn't invented? Should we not honor the contributions fathers make to parenting? For example, fathers often balance many mothers' tendency to

not enforce limits. Fathers often leaven mothers' protective instinct by encouraging reasonable (okay, occasionally not so reasonable) risk-taking.

6. It's time to accept the multi-option man, just as we accept the multi-option woman. We appropriately celebrate women having options other than being a stay-at-home mom. Women absolutely deserve the right to, on the merits, compete for jobs from carpenter to clarinetist to CEO. But we must now legitimate the full range of options for men: from stay-at-home father to 80-hour-a-week scientist. The stay-at-home dad who wants to be a part-time artist should be respected as much as a woman who chooses that option. The man who chooses to work long hours should not be pathologized as a "workaholic" but revered as a hard-working contributor to society. Society, often with the encouragement of the woman in his life, makes men feel, even in today's feminist era, that they must generate most of the family income with a steady ,good paycheck. So he so often suppresses his dreams, for example, of a more creative pursuit, until retirement, by which time he may be too old or sick. This should be the era of the multi-option man as well as of the multi-option woman.

The ultimate irony

Despite all of the above, America is making yet more efforts to exacerbate the anti-male sexism. Last year, President Obama created a well-funded Council on Women and Girls[39] but rejected one on men and boys. Here[40] is that rejected proposal. (Bias alert: I am a member of the commission that created that proposal.) And in Obama's April 6, 2012 speech[41] at the White House Forum on Women and the Economy, he reiterated that he wants to focus yet more on women: "(I) look forward to continuing the important work we are doing to promote the interests of women." After all, women earn 77 cents on the dollar.

America will be better if our goal is merit-based treatment of both men and women.

To comment, click HERE[42].

4
HEALTH CARE REINVENTED
A SYSTEM WE CAN LIVE WITH

You and I are about to start getting our health care in a very different system, defined in a 2,400-page document that even most legislators that passed it didn't read. Can it be implemented effectively enough that when we desperately need it, we'll get timely health care?

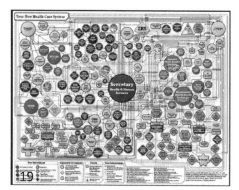

We have reason to be scared

More scary, our health care providers are already overwhelmed: A study[43] reported in the Journal of the American Medical Association reports that 225,000 people a year die as a result of their medical treatments and countless more cases of excess morbidity (unnecessarily long recuperation, unnecessary pain, etc.) occur *every year*. And now, that same number of doctors, nurses, MRIs, operating rooms, etc., will have to care for 40,000,000 more people, who as a group, have high health care needs and will be paying little into the system.

And according to the au courant principle of redistributive "justice," they'll be entitled to the same quality of care as people who pay into the system. Is there something cosmically wrong about people paying into the system putting their lives at greater risk so those who don't pay into the system can get an equal level of health care?.

And the cost? So-called ObamaCare will require employers to provide health care for all its 30+-hour a week employees plus a surcharge to pay for the health care of part-timers, the unemployed. and poor people. Employers claim that that cost on top of all the other employer costs (Social Security, retirement, workers comp, disability, Americans with Disabilities Act, Family and Marriage Leave Act, plus the legal and human costs of defending wrongful termination and other discrimination lawsuits,) will force businesses to eliminate yet more jobs or to go out of business.

When we need it, we have reason to worry that despite paying more for and having less control over our health care, our very lives will be at greater risk.

FreedomCare

I'd place greater faith in what I believe is a better and simpler plan. I call it *FreedomCare:*

1. The indigent would receive free basic care with "basic" defined as: preventive care provided by a nurse practitioner or physician assistant. Major procedures would be subjected to a cost-benefit analysis. For example, a stage-1 cancer patient might receive full treatment, a stage-4 cancer patient only experimental treatments and palliative care. Patients would be allowed to choose their health care providers from among those with room in their schedule but not to go on a waiting list.

2. For the non-indigent, except for catastrophic care, for which insurance could be purchased from the private sector, health care would be paid directly

by the consumer. If consumers had most of the money at stake, 300 million Americans would be exerting the market's invisible hand to drive down costs and improve quality. The good quality, cost-effective providers would succeed, the bad ones driven out of business.

3. To ensure that consumers have the information to choose health care providers and procedures wisely, all doctors, nurses, hospitals, etc., would be required to make key consumer information available, for example, procedures' efficacy rates, cost, patient satisfaction (separately reported by condition,) the provider's risk-adjusted success rates for common procedures, etc.

3a. Insurers would be required to post clear information on coverage, limitations, and price on a well-promoted government website, enabling consumers to easily compare insurance products.

4. Shorten the training of health care providers and make it more practical. That would improve quality while reducing cost and increasing the supply of providers. Currently, our health care providers are trained primarily by professors, who value the theoretical over the practical. Those professors are usually hired and promoted mainly on how much research they produce (almost always in a narrow area, e.g., plantar fasciitis,) not on their ability as a clinician, let alone how effective they are in training clinicians.

Having discussed medical education with a number of physicians, I've become convinced that the status quo, which requires pre-med students to complete courses in organic chemistry, inorganic chemistry, physics, and calculus followed by four years of theory- and arcana-larded medical school (particularly absurd today when so much information is available instantly on the Internet), should be replaced by a two-year practical program taught by master physicians. That would improve patient care while greatly reducing the cost of training a doctor, currently over $200,000 per. (I propose a more modest reinvention of medical education in the next Reinvention.)

FreedomCare would improve quality and access while reducing cost, relatively simply. Compare that with ObamaCare.

To comment, click HERE[44].

5
MEDICAL EDUCATION REINVENTED

Your physician is one of the most important people in your life. Diagnosing and treating you properly can be a matter of life or death.

So it may be disconcerting to know that physicians are trained mainly, not by master clinical physicians, but by research-focused professors. That may partly explain why, according to an article[45] in the Journal of the American Medical Association, 225,000 patients each year die because of their medical treatment, while one in three patients are harmed during a hospital stay. (That number, however, has been disputed[46].)

Professors are better at teaching the cut-and-dried academic science--physics and chemistry, theoretical models, and diagnosis/treatment decision trees-- than the messy but critical subjective parts of medicine: When is it worth subjecting a patient to additional testing or treatment? What would motivate a particular patient to eat broccoli instead of bacon cheeseburgers?

Also, professors too often focus on what they like to teach than on what physicians need to know. For example, is requiring every pre-med student to take a year of physics, a year of organic chemistry, and a year of inorganic chemistry worth the student's time and money? Does requiring such courses weed out students who could become better physicians than students that aced organic chemistry but couldn't motivate an Olympic athlete?

Each item in the curriculum should be subjected to this test: "If students are required to learn this, is there something more important that will go unlearned?"

The more prestigious the medical school, the more likely instruction is to focus on academic and research-related material, not on need-to-know clinical practice. That is because universities acquire prestige far more from their research than from the education they provide. Because lesser-known colleges can't compete with top-tier universities in research, they're more likely to focus on education.

A better way

Dr. Molly Cooke, co-author of the Carnegie Foundation's Educating Physicians: A Call for Reform of Medical School and Residency points to the DeGroote School of Medicine at Canada's McMaster University, which according to its Web site offers "a unique three-year (rather than the usual four) program based on small-group, problem-based study and an early introduction to the clinical experience."

Trim the curriculum so it focuses on what's clinically important, and pre-med and medical education would be both improved and shortened, saving time and money--Currently, the taxpayer spends $9 billion dollars a year merely on residency training[47].

Another weakness of medical education is that, according to Cooke, it encourages hubris. In de-emphasizing the ambiguity and guesswork still necessary in medicine, medical school makes new doctors feel more infallible than they are. Compounding the problem, the arduousness of pre-med programs, medical school, internships and residency create an exaggerated sense of mastery and entitlement. Aspiring physicians must learn mountains of difficult material but too little of it has significant impact on patient outcomes. If physicians' self-appraisal were more realistic, they'd work less condescendingly with other members of the health team. Nurses, social workers, and other allied health professionals often have as much to contribute to patient wellness as do physicians. A medical education that inculcates a measure of humility would help physicians understand the field's current limitations, be more honest with patients and more motivated to contribute their clinical findings to the still adolescent field of medicine.

This brings us to the medical school application and selection process. The selection criteria usually are: GPA (especially in chemistry, biology, and physics,) the Medical College Admission Test (a multiple-choice test of academic science and reasoning), an essay, and volunteer experience. Do those adequately assess a candidate's potential to be a citizen physician, a good listener and someone who could develop enough of a relationship within 12-minute exams to motivate patients to take medication even though it has side effects?

As part of its selection process, the DeGroote School of Medicine has each candidate proceed through six to eight mini interviews[48]. At each one, the candidate is given a simulated problem. For example, the candidate may have to weigh privacy versus safety when the parents of an HIV-infected child say they don't want the diagnosis disclosed to his school. Performance during the simulations is more predictive of interpersonal and communication skills than is the conventional interview.

Alas, the medical school establishment profits from the status quo and has been able to resist change because it controls the oversight entities, for example, the powerful Liaison Committee on Medical Education.

America's current focus on reforming health care should include the reform of medical education. The innovations proposed here would both reduce cost and improve quality, a hard-to-beat combination, especially when it could save your life.

To comment, click HERE[49].

6
DEFENSE REINVENTED

We spend more on defense than anything: The projected defense budget is over $1 *trillion* dollars for 2012 alone!

It's time to take a closer look at whether we'd derive more cost-benefit by reallocating much of the defense spending to other initiatives such as medical and education research, reducing our debt, relieving gridlock, giving to the poor, and returning money to the millions of struggling taxpayers to pump back into the economy as each person sees fit.

As I outlined in this book's Reinvention 1, *any* purchase should be justified mainly by *its cost-benefit versus opportunity cost.* For example, the U.S. maintains hundreds of military bases around the world, from Antigua to Turkey, staffed by 360,000 service members, costing many billions of dollars every year. I believe **we must more rigorously assess, for each base, how much would our safety be reduced if we closed that base or streamlined it to just a handful of software-assisted human monitors. Would the benefit of reallocating that money elsewhere be worth that increase in risk?** I predict that subjecting each defense spending item to that test would result in dramatically reduced military spending.

My vote for the most cost-effective defense expenditure? Expanded conversation with our enemies, including radical groups such as Al Qaeda and the Taliban. Of course, not everything is remediable with discussion. I believe that no conversations with Hitler would have deterred his desire to dominate the world, but the risk/reward and cost/benefit ratios of conversation are good.

In decades past, large defense cuts wouldn't have been as defensible. But today, much of the threat to our security is miniaturized: solo actor terrorists, compact weapons such as suitcase radiologic devices, cyberattacks, bioweapons, etc. Those will not be deterred by massive military bases, battleships, and aircraft bombers. Indeed, such megaweapons often cause much collateral damage, not only to people and property, but to our worldwide reputation. When one of our aerial bombs destroys even one innocent person or home (which is difficult to avoid,) thanks to the Internet, it becomes instant worldwide-disseminable propaganda that is used against us.

My proposed cost-benefit analysis would likely result in the military budget being reduced by hundreds of billions of dollars *every year,* which could be reallocated to more cost-beneficial initiatives, including reducing our debt. The latter, in itself, could improve our national security more than all the B-2 bombers.

To comment, click HERE[50].

7
JUSTICE REINVENTED

Imagine you've just been sued. Unless it's a small claim, you usually end up hiring a lawyer to fight your opponent's lawyer. Or if you're poor, you hope you'll get a contingency-paid or pro-bono attorney able to compete with your opponent's high-priced one. Not a good feeling.

Our revered but deeply flawed system

Our justice system is expensive, time-consuming, and subject to ethical excesses by lawyers who are rewarded not for furthering justice but for winning.

Too, you may worry that an attorney will be tempted to drag out the proceedings to make more money or exhaust you into giving up: presenting every bit of even unimportant evidence, making non-essential motions, etc. Often, attorney games-playing and court system backups can mean years until your dispute is resolved. The process's variable length makes the cost hard to predict and thus difficult to decide whether it's worth litigating.

And litigation's outcome too often depends on whether you hired a better attorney than did your opponent, which, on average, hurts the poor. Our system of justice is, alas, not blind.

Of course, the status-quo advocacy system has a rationale: that the clash of advocates' ideas helps the important arguments to emerge. But is that a dispositive argument?

A Solution: Dispute Resolution Centers

Here, I advocate pilot-testing an alternative: Dispute Resolution Centers, a one-stop shop where it's easier for disputants to select the most cost-effective option for their situation: counseling, mediation, arbitration, traditional adversarial trial, or *non-adversarial trial.* Cost would be a per-hour fee, with a sliding scale for modest-to-low-income people, with the subsidy, as in the current system, paid by the taxpayer.

The non-adversarial trial requires explanation. First, know that its use has precedent. In the U.S., non-adversarial trials are used in arbitration, traffic violations, administrative law cases, and small claims courts, and more broadly in other countries, notably France, Russia, China, and the Ukraine.

Here's how I envision non-adversarial trials best working. Depending on how much the disputants want to spend, there would, at minimum, be a judge/investigator, charged with investigating the facts and law and with rendering a judgment. At maximum, there would be multiple investigators, (lawyers with supplemental training as investigators) each charged with unearthing the relevant facts and law, not advocating for one side, a jury making the decision, and a judge presiding to ask questions and to instruct the jury. In criminal matters, a jury would be required.

In a non-adversarial trial, justice is more likely to be served because instead of two lawyers being paid on whether they win, their goal would be to seek the truth and their pay would be based on how well and cost-effectively they do so.

A side benefit of using non-adversarial trials is that the field of law would attract people motivated more by a desire for justice than for winning. Today, too often, people are attracted to being a lawyer because they like to win arguments.

Because all dispute resolution options would be available in one-stop Dispute Resolution Centers, disputants could more easily find the right approach, and if the disputants couldn't agree on one, a judge would decide.

In addition to facilitating options other than expensive, too-often unjust advocate-based trials, Dispute Resolution Centers would reduce the huge backlog of trial cases. Timely justice might become less of an oxymoron.

Yet another advantage of the model I'm proposing is that, currently, organizations too often use an arbitrator or mediator who regularly does business with that organization and so has reason to side with it. In the model proposed, there would not be such "preferred providers."

I advocate here for pilot study to evaluate Dispute Resolution Centers versus the traditional system. A pilot might have the Dispute Resolution Centers consider only civil matters or both civil and criminal ones. Also, a study might compare public versus private versions of Dispute Resolution Centers. In that, disputants would be allowed to choose public or private dispute resolution services, just as we allow people to choose public or private schools and public or private hospitals.

Of course, the status quo is always difficult to change, especially something as long-standing and foundational as our advocate-based legal system. But just as many of us bristle against people who insist on strict interpretation of the 224-year-old Constitution rather than adapting it to fit today's circumstances, is it not time to at least pilot-test what may be a wiser path to justice?

To comment, click HERE[51].

8
TAXATION REINVENTED

A poll[52] by The Economist finds that 62 percent say the tax system needs a major overhaul.

Soak the rich more?

An often recommended approach is to soak the rich more. After all, the rich-poor gap is wide. In addition, no matter how smart, hard-working or innovative someone is, or how many jobs he or she creates, it seems cosmically unjust that some people own a mansion (or two), yacht (or two) and more money than they could spend in Methuselah's lifetime, while other people must eat ramen in hovels. Also making me sympathetic to squeezing fat cats is that the poor spend a larger percentage of their income, so redistributing dollars to them quickly pumps money into the economy.

On the other hand, I am not immune to opposing arguments, for example, that the top 5% pay 59% of the federal income tax[53], and that taking money from the rich to give to the poor punishes the innovators and job creators and rewards people who are not, and we'll get more of what we reward, less of what we punish. Plus, money left in the hands of the rich will create more jobs and more innovations--from disease cures to iPhone5--than if Robin-Hooded.

As a result, I am agnostic on the wisdom of redistributive "justice."

The Case for Replacing Income Tax with Sales Tax

The change in our tax system that I believe would most benefit America is to replace our federal, state, and local income taxes with a sales tax.

In 2004 testimony to the House Ways and Means Oversight subcommittee, University of Michigan professor Joel Slemrod estimated that Americans spend at least $135 billion[54] annually on tax record-keeping and return preparation, In 2011, a Laffer Foundation study[55] indicated that Slemrod was too conservative: It estimated $431 billion, an extra 30 cents on top of every dollar we pay in taxes. We're all eager to find a way to get back even a few minutes in our day and a few extra dollars in our wallet. Imagine if all that money and time we spend on tax record-keeping and preparing were returned to us.

Another problem with income tax is that underpayment is rife. The IRS reported that in 2006, the most recent year available, Americans underreported[56] $450 billion, up by 1/3 from just five years earlier. An IRS report[57] released in 2012 found that tens of thousands of federal employees, including in the White House, collectively underpaid billions of dollars. Alas, in our system, cheaters too often win.

In place of income tax, I'd substitute a sales tax with basic items exempted to ensure the poor pay relatively little, plus a luxury tax to ensure the rich pay their fair share. The luxury tax would not be set so high as to significantly grow the black market.

What constitutes "basic items?" I'd want to test whether exempting non-luxury food, clothing, and cars under $5,000 would result in low- and moderate-income people paying more or less tax than they now pay in income tax.

The sales-tax rate would be reduced by:

• including Internet sales as taxable, which would allow local businesses to compete on a level playing field

• legalizing and then taxing prostitution

• heavily taxing alcohol and tobacco, because consumption of both products impose heavy burdens on people, their families, and on the health care system.

Because of those, I'm guessing (wildly) that the revenue-neutral federal sales tax rate could be around 10 percent plus an additional 4% state and local. Add to that the existing state and local sales taxes, and I'm guessing the total sales tax would end up at about 25%, of course, with basic items exempt.

Advantages of sales tax versus income tax:

- Less time and money spent on tax record-keeping and income tax reporting. Unlike with the income tax, individuals would not have to keep tax records nor file income tax returns. Currently, 150 million Americans must file an often complicated federal tax return, a state tax return, and in hundreds of cities, counties, and school districts[58], a local income tax return.

  And under my proposal, retailers would have little additional work. I propose a unified sales tax form: each retailer would submit sales information on one form, one copy to the IRS, another to the state, another to any local taxing authority, just as our W-2 forms currently do. Of course, states and locales could, as currently, set their own tax rates.

- Less cheating. Of course, as with state sales tax, some people manage to avoid tax by buying in the black market, but much less money would likely be lost to cheating than the aforementioned $450 billion every year lost just to federal income tax underpayment.

  Some academics prefer a value-added tax (VAT) to a sales tax because it's even more fraud-resistant, but a VAT likely requires[59] as much paperwork as an income tax. Also, a VAT taxes not just products but services, which, for reasons stated in the next two bullets, is undesirable.

- Sales tax hits consumption instead of income. That means we'll consume less and thus decrease the national carbon footprint.

- Consumer spending would likely be reallocated from taxable *products* to not-sales-taxed *services*: from new mom aide to homework helper to personal errand-doer/concierge to technology demystifier to elder companion.

  If we spend more on such services than, for example, on yet another pair of shoes, our national quality of life should improve. And reallocating spending from products to services would create good, offshore-resistant jobs. While most jobs such as tutor or personal assistant would be part-time, two or three of them could comprise a reasonable living and a career that many people would consider more rewarding than manufacturing or distributing said shoes.

Of course, if consumption of products declines, some jobs will be lost in production, tax accounting, and other sectors. But just as most people wouldn't justify the tobacco industry because it creates jobs, that shouldn't justify retaining a high-consumption society or the need for so many accountants and auditors: currently, 1.2 million[60].

So if I were allowed to make one change in our taxation system, it would be to replace the income tax with sales tax.:

Other reinventions of taxation

But I also propose these changes:

If additional taxation of high-income earners were deemed wise, I'd advocate a *ground tax,* which would require landowners to pay a federal surcharge on the land portion of their property tax. That's minimally game-able, doesn't require recordkeeping, and doesn't penalize land owners for improving their property.

To spur investment, which would, in turn, boost innovation and create jobs, I'd only lightly tax interest, dividends, and capital gains. Investment income under $5,000 a year would remain untaxed. That rate would rise to 15 percent at $40,000 plus. It's likely that a majority of Americans believe it is fair that people who earn money without working for it should have that income taxed.

I'd increase the estate tax. There is something cosmically wrong about people receiving a fortune by birthright. I envision the first $100,000 remaining untaxed and the estate tax rate would accelerate to 65 percent on inheritance over $1,000,000.

With regard to payroll taxes, the plan would retain Social Security for the poor, which would be paid for by the national sales tax. However, Social Security would be phased out for everyone else. Despite the hefty 10.4 percent Social Security tax on earnings up to $110,000[61], the payout is low and the program is at risk of bankruptcy. Of course, if Social Security were phased out, some taxpayers would lose but, overall, it may be wise to leave that huge amount of money in taxpayers' pockets to spend or invest as they see fit. The phasing-out should be gradual to reduce taxpayer disgruntlement and lawsuits.

To comment, click HERE[62].

9
INVESTING REINVENTED

Especially in tight times, whatever savings we have should be invested wisely. That benefits us not only as individuals, it means that worthy recipients get our investments, which leads to a better America.

Fortunately, investing wisely is far easier than financial advisers--who make their money by making us feel we need them--would have us believe.

Even many sophisticated investment advisers agree that the following no-brains-required strategy is likely to, over the long run, yield better results than most investors obtain using strategies that are far more time-consuming, anxiety-provoking, and requiring great expertise or paying a hefty fee to a financial adviser.

1. Keep an amount equal to six months living expenses in one of the nation's highest yielding bank CDs or money market funds. How do you find them? Easy: bankrate.com lists them daily. It feels great to see your savings grow. It's like magic--you earn interest on your interest. That's a guarantee you'll make money without having to do a thing--and with bank CDs and money market funds, the risk is extremely low.

1a. If you're in the top federal tax bracket, you might be better off in a Vanguard tax-exempt bond fund[63] than in a bank CD or money market fund.

2. Keep most of your money in a low-cost, no-load mutual fund. They offer much greater potential rewards than a bank CD albeit with greater risk. I am not a licensed financial advisor, but what makes most sense to me is a Vanguard All-in-One Fund[64]. Those come in different flavors depending on your risk tolerance and how long you anticipate keeping your money invested. But all all-in-one funds invest in a mix of stocks and bonds, many of which have international exposure, so your savings are not tied just to the U.S. economy. And Vanguard's fees are among the very lowest in the industry.

2a. If you're in the top federal tax bracket (the 35% rate), you might be better off in a tax-managed fund such as the Vanguard Tax-Managed Capital Appreciation Fund[65] or the less aggressive Vanguard Tax-Managed Balanced Fund[66].

Do *not* try to time the market--most try and fail. Instead, every time you have an extra $500-$2,500 to invest, do so that day. That way, your money goes to work for you immediately. Also, that automatically buys you more shares when prices are low, fewer when prices are high.

I believe that all citizens should be taught the above model of investing. It would likely result in more net income for the public, more confidence that it's worth saving for a rainy day, a greater sense of security, something we could all use in these insecure times, and more money going to worthy recipients, which leads to a better America.

Disclaimer: I am not a professional investment adviser and thus am not giving investment advice here. This merely is a model I've used in my investing. Also, except for the bank CDs, note that these are uninsured investments and subject to loss. Lastly, I am not affiliated with Vanguard and have nothing to gain from your investing in it.

To comment, click HERE[67].

10
HOUSING REINVENTED

If, as many predict, the economy continues to struggle, fewer people will be able to afford to rent let alone to buy a decent-sized place to live.

Factory homes. We should expand use of factory-built homes[68], alternately called modular housing, and in years past, pre-fab houses.

For the most part, we still build homes as we did 100 years ago, stick by stick, pipe by pipe, tile by tile. Not only is that cost-ineffective, it too often results in poorly constructed homes.

Today's versions of factory-built homes aren't your parents' prefabs. They can be, well, fab. You can pick from countless models, from basic to luxurious (see above,) designed by architects you couldn't afford if the cost weren't amortized across a design's many customers.

And because the home is stamped out in a factory, it both costs less and is likely to be of higher quality. Conventional site-based construction requires construction workers rather than industrial machines trying to precisely cut and correctly install all those pieces of wood, sheetrock, pipes, and wire.

And with a factory-built home, it's just weeks before you can move into your new home with all the finishes you've selected.

Peter Christiansen of South San Francisco said, "I have lived in a factory-built house for the past 13 years. It's one bedroom, 600 sq. feet, next to BART and Kaiser, and just two miles from the ocean. The house cost me $22,500 13 years ago. I pay $650 a month "space rent," which is on the high end, even for the Bay Area."

Better soundproofing. One reason many people feel the need to spend the additional money on a free-standing home rather than on a condo or apartment is the noise from the neighbors and the street: multi-unit buildings are more likely to be located on a busy street. And of course, the millions of people who can't afford to buy a home even if they wanted to, would appreciate more quiet and being able to be as noisy as *they* like. A solution is greater use of the new generation of sound-dampening drywall, for example, QuietRock[69], flooring, for example QuietBarrier[70], and windows, for example, Citiquiet[71].

Affinity housing. Another way to reduce living costs, of course, is to live with others. Alas, finding a compatible roommate isn't easy nor is returning home to live with your family. So America should have more affinity housing, as we do with housing developments for people 55+. There could be homes for people interested in, for example, the arts, pacifism, the medical profession, or who have a physical condition, from triathlete to cancer patient.

Roommatematch.com. It would be like Match.com for roommates. With today's lousy economy, it's not just people just starting out who are willing to live with roommates. For example, there are the four million homeowners who, in just the last four years, have lost their home to foreclosure.

A fairer idea for welfare housing. Why not have welfare recipients live as college students do: two or three to a small room, cafeteria-style food, etc., with social services provided, for example, parenting education, GED classes, computer training, drug/alcohol counseling, etc.? That would save taxpayer money, make services convenient, and provide a privacy incentive to get off welfare. **If dorm-style living is good enough for Harvard students, it should be good enough for welfare recipients.**

SuperSublet.com. While they're at work, millions of people leave their home or apartment vacant, unused, for eight or more hours a day. At the same time, countless businesses, from individual counselors to mega-corporations, build or lease space for offices, meeting rooms, classrooms, etc.

Why not pair them up? Here are some advantages:

- Rather than renting or building sterile office space, SuperSublet.com would make it easy for a counselor, corporation, university, etc. to find a more pleasant apartment or home to rent.
- It would likely cost less because the resident had otherwise expected to get zero dollars.
- It's an unexpected easy source of income for the resident.
- It's green: less building reduces the carbon footprint.

Of course, there are obstacles. Government would have to relax zoning regulations. Insurance companies would have to offer riders on renters and homeowners policies. And landlords would have to accept the sublessees. Perhaps, just as hotels charge an extra fee for guests with pets, landlords might charge an additional "wear-and-tear" fee for tenants who wish to sublet. That way, your home can be   where your heart and cash cow are.

To comment, click <u>HERE</u>[72].

11
TRANSPORTATION REINVENTED

Yes, Americans love their cars, and with good reason: Plunking yourself down into the sanctuary of your car, with a comfy seat and temperature adjusted just where you like it, you get to leave precisely when you want to go precisely where you want, point-to-point.

Compare that against mass transit. You typically must walk or drive to get to the train or bus station, try to find a parking spot, wait for a bus or train, deal with the discomfort of being crowded into a mass conveyance, too often exacerbated by loud or even physically threatening youths. You must wait for each stop, and on arrival at your stop, perhaps take another bus or train. Door-to-door time can be twice as long as driving. Especially in our ever busier, more stressful lives, being pressured to endure mass transit is just not a satisfactory transportation solution for most people.

The flying car. My favorite alternative to building more roads is the flying car. Because it could fly anywhere, not just on a road, creating a flying car is the equivalent of creating dozens of times the current number of freeways and other roads for free. The flying car would take off vertically, so no airport is required. Lest you think this is a Jetsons-cartoon-like fantasy, <u>two that still do require a runway are already in production</u>[73]. This suggests that within a decade (the time these days it takes to get a freeway approved and built) a mass-affordable, safe, vertical-takeoff, flying car could be available.

Smarter road building. In the interim, I believe we must *not* focus on mass transit and instead, build more roads and add lanes. We simply cannot ask people to sit in ever greater gridlock, while their idling cars spew ever more pollutants.

However, more effort needs to be made to innovate in freeway construction, for example, factory-prebuilt road sections (like sections of model train tracks), constructed of a nanotech-designed (honeycomb?) amalgam of recycled materials. The modules would be shipped by truck from factory to the road site and laid, one next to another. Compared with conventional road building, that would be cheaper and faster, avoiding the years of traffic delays that occur every time even one new lane is added.

An alternative to toll plazas. Toll plazas, even with transponder toll-paying, greatly increases traffic congestion. An answer: Eliminate toll plazas and in counties containing toll roads, bridges, or tunnels, add a fee added to each driver's annual car registration. Some would argue that would be unfair to drivers who don't those roads, but all our taxes pay for services we may not use, welfare, for example. The benefit far outweighs the unfairness.

A breathalizer ignition lock. *Every year,* 13,000 people die in vehicle accidents caused by under-the-influence. Countless more are injured. I advocate that all steering wheels be required to contain an breathalizer that, if the person is under the influence, locks the car's engine. They are already available[74] for alcohol. A device should be developed for marijuana.

Glow-in-the-dark bicycle frames. Bicycles, mopeds, and motorcycles are cost-effective, energy-saving alternatives to the car but their use is limited, in part because of safety. Among the biggest safety problems is that drivers fail to see two-wheel vehicles, especially at night. So I propose that all two-wheeled vehicles be required to have strips of reflective tape affixed to their frames. HERE[75] is an example.

Raise CAFE standards. I would raise CAFE (Corporate Average Fuel Economy) standards so that every vehicle manufacturer's fleet of cars and light trucks would, by 2025, average 100 miles per gallon. (Automakers have already agreed to 50 mpg[76].)

Yes, that would mean that until a breakthrough technology arrives, more new cars would be small, which would cause some increase in car crash injuries.

But that liability is outweighed by the advantages of a high-gas-mileage America, especially compared with more onerous approaches to energy-independent, low-carbon transportation. In addition to abetting energy independence and decreasing carbon footprint, the 100 mpg mandate would mean our cost-per-driving mile would dramatically decrease because of the better gas mileage and because the lower demand for gas would force oil companies to cut the price. Those cost savings benefit all of us significantly, particularly the poor--and with 100% certitude.

Driving is freedom and so it shouldn't be unduly restricted, especially when there are more potent and less burdensome approaches to energy independence and clean air.

To comment, click <u>HERE</u>[77].

12
THE PUBLIC LIBRARY, REINVENTED

Most library space has long been devoted to books. But, of course, ever more of our reading more conveniently comes from the internet: downloaded books, audios, and videos, Googled articles, online dictionary lookups, etc. So today, there are better uses of library space than labyrinths of bookshelves.

Most of a library's book holdings should be purchased as e-books, freeing up most of a library's space. Ebook readers could be lent or even given to patrons. Popular books should be retained in print.

Converting libraries into community centers

How to best use the resulting increase in available library space? Libraries should transition into community centers. Already, of course, libraries have speakers, children's puppeteers, etc., but much more can occur, for example,

- hourly, citizen-run town hall meetings on a topic du jour, perhaps with coffee, pastries, sandwiches, and salads sold.
- a meeting place. Most people feel relaxed and positive in a library. That makes it a good place for negotiations and other meetings, for example, contract negotiations between union and management.
- Starting when libraries normally close, say 9 pm, the library could become a cafe/non-alcoholic nightclub with library-consistent entertainment that has wide appeal: folk guitarist, poetry reading, etc.

Convert librarians from information pointers to information gatherers

Probably most important, librarians should expand their role from just telling patrons where to find information to gathering that information, at least for non-students.

For example, librarians could work from home, with access to the library's expanded resources including proprietary databases too expensive for individuals to own. The librarian could respond to emailed and phoned requests, for example, from a patron who has just been diagnosed with a disease and isn't a good researcher. The librarian could cut and paste best articles, pictures, videos, etc. into an email sent to the patron. Depending on the nature of the question, the librarian's answer can be added to an online worldwide database for others to reference and improve upon in the future. It's a wiser use of taxpayer dollars to fund librarians as information retrievers than to fund the acquisition and storage of a library-size book collection.

To comment, click HERE[78].

13
OUR APPROACH TO THE ISRAELI/PALESTINIAN CONFLICT, REINVENTED

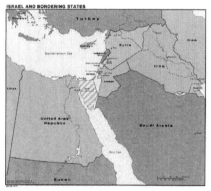

In defending Israel, the U.S. spends a fortune, endangers our supply of Middle East oil, and incites terrorists. There's a better solution.

A 3,000-year enmity is unlikely to heal

For thousands of years, Jews and Arabs have been unable to live peacefully side by side. How naive for the United Nations to have placed Israel so it is surrounded by the massively larger Arab world. (Israel is the sliver in the map's center.)

The Israelis, from Day One, aspired to and succeeded in becoming a modern, largely secular democracy. It has created the highest per-capita rate of health and tech innovations.[79] Although Jews are only 1/5 of 1% of the world's population, 20% of the Nobel Prize winners since 1900 are Jewish.[80]

Meanwhile, while much of the surrounding Arab/Muslim world lives much as it did the Dark Ages, for example, with extreme fundamentalism required on penalty of death, with women in burkas, where children are taught they will get to have sex with 41 virgins if they strap dynamite to themselves and blow up a Jewish cafe and all the people in it.

Can we be optimistic that these two cultures, enemies for millennia, will live side-by-side in enduring peace? In a world in which the surrounding countries, far larger, are fully accepted as all-Muslim states but Israel is told that its tiny sliver of land cannot be an all-Jewish state, an island of safety from millennia of attempts to destroy the Jewish people: from Ancient Rome through the Inquisition, from the pogroms to the Holocaust, and, from the moment the United Nations gave Israel that sliver of desert, continued bombardment from Muslim entities?

And the trend is accelerating. The Palestinian people made their intentions toward Israel clear when it elected Hamas to be its government, a terrorist group whose very charter calls for the destruction of Israel, and since then has steadily increased its bombings of Israel. And the president of nuclear Iran calls for Israel's obliteration.

New Israel

I believe the best solution to the Palestinian/Israeli conflict is for another country with ample unused land such as the U.S., Canada, or Australia to offer an Israel-sized sliver of low-value land as the *New Israel*.

As a child of Holocaust survivors, I, better than many, understand that many Israelis would find it difficult to trade their historical homeland for a new one, but to save lives and a fortune of money, and ensure ongoing peace, I believe it is a compromise worth making.

One reasonable choice for New Israel's location would be a sliver of the low-cost forest land 50 to 100 miles north of New York City, the city with the largest concentration of Jews, and a country in which anti-Semitism is relatively low. Countries set aside much larger swaths merely to protect wildlife, so it is reasonable to assume that at least one country would offer a sliver to protect humans. That is especially likely because the donor country would become an instant worldwide hero for solving the age-old Arab-Israeli conflict, thereby reducing the global threat of Islamic terrorism.

Plus, New Israel would become that country's deeply indebted ally. That is significant because Israel is, for example, an acknowledged world leader in how to defend against terrorism, something, alas, of ever increasing importance. Also, Israel has the world's #1 per-capita rate of medical and biotech patents.

Of course, it's possible that no country would give that sliver to the Israelis. After all, Franklin Delano Roosevelt refused even to accept a ship of Holocaust victims during World War II. But I believe the chances of a country donating that sliver are far greater than the chances of Arabs and

Israelis, for decade after decade, living peacefully side-by-side.

How would it work? All Israeli citizens would be given the *option* to move to New Israel. Low-income people could get help with moving expenses. The World Bank, G-8, or other consortium would fund that. Of course, some Israelis would elect to remain in Israel but, over time, many would emigrate to New Israel or other countries. That would peaceably transition the current Israel/Palestine into a Palestinian-run state with too few Jews to engender significant conflict.

During the discussion at a Passover Seder, consensus was that further dialogue is the best path to peace. But the Israelis and Arabs have dialogued for 60 years, indeed 3,000 years--and the result has been an *increase* in enmity. And time is the Israelis' enemy. The Palestinian birthrate is much greater than the Israelis' and while Israeli schoolchildren are being educated in the importance of peace, Palestinian children are encouraged to become suicide bombers.

I'd sooner bet on New Israel as a path to peace than on overcoming a 3,000-year-long enmity.

To comment, click HERE[81].

14
OUR APPROACH TO CLIMATE CHANGE, REINVENTED

The science is *not* yet clear enough to justify the massive costs of attempting to cool the planet.

You might ask, "How can you say that. After all, the UN's International Panel on Climate Change (IPCC) says it's true."

Fact is, only a few scientists on the IPCC have the power to contribute substantially to their documents and it's a stacked group--scientists ideologically predisposed to major spending to attempt to cool the planet. As documented below, there are enough credible dissenters to justify a debate on the wisdom of our current and planned massive spending and incursions to human freedoms to attempt to cool the planet.

The data, the probabilities, a cost-benefit analysis

When one looks dispassionately at the data on climate change, it would seem that more and better data are needed before making a massive commitment to try to cool the planet. Remember, to justify the huge costs, all of six things must be true:

- The planet is warming (estimated probability =.9)

  Nobel Prize Winner, Ivar Giaever, in resigning from the American Physical Society on Sep. 13, 2011, wrote this:

  Dear Ms. Kirby

  Thank you for your letter inquiring about my membership. I did not renew it because I can not live with the statement below:

  > "Emissions of greenhouse gases from human activities are changing the atmosphere in ways that affect the Earth's climate. Greenhouse gases include carbon dioxide as well as methane, nitrous oxide and other gases. They are emitted from fossil fuel combustion and a range of industrial and agricultural processes. **The evidence is incontrovertible**: Global warming is occurring. If no mitigating actions are taken, significant disruptions in the Earth's physical and ecological systems, social systems, security and human health are likely to occur. We must reduce emissions of greenhouse gases beginning now."

  In the APS it is ok to discuss whether the mass of the proton changes over time and how a multi-universe behaves, but the evidence of global warming is **incontrovertible**? The claim (how can you measure the average temperature of the whole earth for a whole year?) is that the temperature has changed from ~288.0 to ~288.8 degree Kelvin in about 150 years, which (if true) means to me is that the temperature has been amazingly stable, and both human health and happiness have definitely improved in this 'warming' period.

  Ivar Giaever, Nobel Laureate

- The warming is substantially man-made (probability = .9) The consensus is that it is, but and a recent study[82] reported in the *Wall Street Journal* from the respected European Organization for Nuclear

Research CERN, finds that global warming is primarily *not* manmade.

-
- The warming's net effect must be so negative (for example, outweighing the benefits to cold climates) as to justify the cost. (probability = .8)
- The science underpinning the plan to cool the planet must actually be valid. (probability = .8) The scientific consensus is that it is, but no less than top scientists MIT's Richard Lindzen[83], Harvard's Willie Wei-Hock Soon[84], Princeton's Freeman Dyson[85], and many less well-known but credible scientists are convinced that the computer models are based on dubious assumptions. That too is the conclusion of Climate Change Reconsidered[86], a 430-page report written by 11 scientists.
- Here's a key one: The world's 200 nations must all substantially comply with the with the greatly increased costs and severe incursions of freedom that the effort to cool the planet would require. This must be true not just in the short term, but for the 50-100 years until alternatives to fossil fuels advance enough. (probability = .2)
- And another key one: The money and human resources spent to cool the planet is better spent than on anything else they might have been spent on. (probability = .2)

The joint probability of all those occurring is 2%.[2]

When we endorse the plan to try to cool the planet, for that roughly 2%-probability event, we accept the 100% probability that we will spend a fortune we don't have and impose great restrictions on our freedom--for example, forcing us to sit in gridlock (ironically, spewing pollutants) because environmentalists have blocked most freeway construction. For example, most "stimulus" money has been focused on mass transit, which, for most people, is usually more time-consuming and less comfortable than the sanctuary of our car.

To attempt to cool the planet, we are spending a fortune and imposing great restrictions on our freedom--for example, forcing us to sit in gridlock (ironically, spewing pollutants) because environmentalists have blocked most freeway construction. For example, most "stimulus" money has been focused on mass transit, which is usually time-consuming and less comfortable than

---

[2] Of course, those probabilities are conjectural but all projections in this area are because there are so many variables that cannot be adequately measured or predicted

the sanctuary of our car. Most of the spending on roads is not to build new roads or lanes but merely to re-pave roads, a usually non-essential project that not only costs us precious tax dollars, but forces us to sit in more traffic during the seemingly-endless construction process.

A plea for debate

The reinvention I ask for is not, "Don't worry about global warming." It is for scientists, the media, and all of us to recognize that there are responsible research-backed policy recommendations other than "The world is doomed unless we spend, virtually without limits, to attempt to cool the planet." These narratives are worth comparing against the IPCC's.

We need to replace the censorship of responsible dissent with a careful consideration of it. It's time for research and for debate, not yet for enviro-religious fervor and massive spending. There may be too many surer ways to spend money and effort to improve humankind, for example, immunizing children in developing countries, better funding research on sudden heart attack, and improving education so it lives up to its yet unrealized potential.

To comment, click HERE[87].

15
THE ECONOMY REINVENTED

I believe that capitalism, socialism, and even a hybrid--what I call *cushioned capitalism*-- are inadequate economic systems:

Capitalism has winners and many losers, too many of whom end up destitute. And because it takes ever more brainpower, drive, and often technical expertise to be one of capitalism's winners, merely urging low achievers to "buck up and work harder" is likely to work ever less well.

Socialism is flawed because, as Margaret Thatcher said, "Eventually you run out of other people's money." Also, socialism rewards low achievers and punishes, through "progressive" taxation, the segment of the population that contributes most to society. Already, the top 5% of earners pay 59% of the income taxes[88].

Even cushioned capitalism---capitalism with a generous safety net, is problematic. It's merely a compromise between two deeply flawed economic systems.

Simplism: An alternative

Of course, many countries use a capitalism/socialism hybrid but I believe there's a better approach. I call it *Simplism.* It requires educating the public about three things:

1. The wisdom of our buying personal services rather than non-essential products. Our lives benefit more from such services as a tutor for our kids, assistant for ourselves, or a companion for our elders than from buying jewelry, new cars every few years, expensive vacations, big houses, etc.

Of course, if the public was less materialistic, many jobs creating and distributing those goods would be lost, disproportionately to low-skill/low motivation workers. So for Simplism to work, I believe the government would need to create taxpayer-funded jobs for those unable to hold a private sector job. These jobs might include, under supervision, building housing, assisting in classrooms, cleaning up blighted neighborhoods, etc.

2. By reducing our spending to the truly important, we'd gain greater benefits than what our purchases would have generated: We'd gain the freedom to do the sorts of work we want, the time to pursue our desired non-remunerative pursuits, and the peace of mind that comes from the absence of big unpaid bills.

3. The importance of considering learning to be an entrepreneur, to run your own business. That avoids your needing to be a wage slave, paid as little as the employer can get away with, provides greater job security than if employed by others, and brings to the public better, faster, or less expensive products and services, thereby improving all of our lives. And of course, creating a new business creates new jobs.

The skill of entrepreneurship may be as important as the 3 Rs. Therefore, I believe it should be taught in high schools and colleges as well as through entrepreneurship boot camps available to all.

An Even Bigger Change

A serious flaw shared by both capitalism and socialism is that their unit of currency is money.

As a thought experiment, here I propose an economic system in which everyone is paid the same: enough to live in a modest apartment, drive a modest car, have modest health care, etc. And to increase people's motivation to work hard in school, pursue a challenging career, work hard on the job etc, people would be rewarded not with extra cash, but with *Contribution Points.*

Already, many if not most people do much work for no money because they feel they're making a contribution: They volunteer for a favorite cause, they write reviews on Yelp, they contribute their time to improving crowd-created products such as Wikipedia or Firefox. Part of many people's motivation is to get points: for example, toward being a high-ranked Amazon reviewer, even though those points aren't redeemable for anything.

In a *Contribution-Points-based economy*, anyone who wanted to participate would add their name to a new website; let's call it ContributionPoints.org. Then, anyone could award Contribution Points to anyone else, just as we all can review a book on Amazon and "Recommend" someone or something on Facebook. People would award points on a scale such as -100 (selling crack to children) to +100 (inventing something that helps many people.) For example, a child doing his homework one night might earn one or two points.

Thus instead of competing for dollars, people would be competing for how much societal contribution they've made. I believe that would immeasurably improve our world.

Of course, the system as I propose needs a lot of work. For example, the system would need to address such problems as, "How often should someone award a person who's working 60 hours a week for decades trying to cure cancer?" and "Should public figures be excluded?" After all, their fans would bestow many points each time a rock star merely opens her mouth on the radio or mp3 player? But if we exclude famous people, we exclude some of society's greatest contributors. And of course, the system would be subject to abuse just as, for example, a hotel owner might write a false bad TripAdvisor.com review of a competing hotel. Would average folks be demotivated by seeing in a number, that despite their best efforts, their contribution to society was deemed much smaller than that of others?

Clearly, the model needs work. But I predict that when day is done, some version of a contribution point system plus the self-regulating power of crowd-sourcing would, *net,* result in people's contribution-point total being a more worthy measure of how well they're living their life than the number of dollars in their bank account.

And importantly, I believe that a person's point total being public would be a strong motivator to him or her. Nearly all of us care how we are perceived by others. Our contribution-points score would be a measure of that. I hypothesize that a person's score would be a greater source of pride than what many people do in a money-based economy to feel proud and impress: buy designer-label clothes, drive fancy cars, buy a house in a tony neighborhood, etc.

Of course, getting the public to embrace a contribution-points-based economy would require a massive education effort, but education has made remarkable changes, for example dramatically increasing the literacy rate. So is it absurd to think we might get sufficient embracing of a contribution-point-based society if our major mind molders--the schools, colleges, media, government, and religious institutions--undertook a major effort to help people realize that the value of one's life lies in how contributory it is?

I am well aware that this is a pie-and-the-sky idea and that this germinal proposal needs much improvement. That's why I'm asking for your reactions. But I believe that big, new, nascent ideas are a worthy ingredient in our recipe for building a better world.

To comment, click HERE[89].

REINVENTIONS OF WORK

16
CREATING GOOD JOBS

Today, creating jobs is Job One, and I worry that current plans will fail. Here are reasons why:

People Don't Just Need Jobs. They Need Good Jobs.

- Both sides of the aisle advocate extending 99-week employment checks to more people, on the belief that redistributing money to people likely to spend rather than save it, will thereby create jobs. Alas, that has a serious side effect. Nearly all my unemployed clients, in the confidentiality of my office, admit that each time unemployment payments are extended, they feel less pressure to look for a job. They're just sitting around.

- We've already tried massive stimulus and it created few jobs. It's oft been lamented, "The job stimulus didn't stimulate and those shovel-ready jobs weren't." That doesn't inspire sufficient confidence that it's worth spending another trillion or two trillion(!) of our tax dollars.

- Funding jobs with taxpayer dollars means taking money from the taxpayers (those most likely to use money to create jobs) and redistributing it to those less likely to.

- Once any government-stimulus-spending-created jobs are completed, more taxpayer-funded money will likely be required to keep the recipients employed.

- Many of the infrastructure jobs are make-work. For example, when politicians say spending will be on roads, they don't say they'll be *building* roads, which would relieve congestion. Environmental activists are making that very difficult. Instead, the road money heavily goes to repaving existing roads. I don't know what's going on nationwide, but where I'm driving, I'm seeing the stimulus-funded repaving work being done on roads that really don't need repaving, certainly not enough to justify the cost to the taxpayer. The main result is that I'm forced to sit in more traffic because of the repaving work going on, and which seems to take far longer than it should.

A Better Jobs Plan

I believe that just the following two ideas would create millions of enduring, pro-social, offshore-resistant jobs.

Entrepreneurship Nation

Both sides of the aisle agree that government stimulus spending, at best, is a jump-start, that permanent job creation must come from the private sector. Most people also agree that entrepreneurs, while providing better, faster, cheaper goods and services, also create jobs.

So why not replace just a fraction of our arcana-larded K-16 curriculum with entrepreneurship education? For example, most high school students spend many hours deriving geometric theorems, balancing chemical equations, memorizing historical facts, and deciphering Shakespearian language. Could it be reasonably be argued that all those are more important for all students than learning how to start and run an ethical yet successful business?

While some entrepreneurs are born not made, much is learnable, especially if taught *not* by ivory-tower academics but by successful, ethical businesspeople. I imagine that many, especially the retired successful businesspeople, would be willing to do that even as a volunteer.

America Assists

It's widely agreed that buying non-essential "stuff" is unlikely to lead to happiness. Don't we all know people who live in an impressive home, who replace their good used car with a new one, go on costly vacations, and buy lots of la-di-dah clothes and jewelry, yet after a brief shopper's high, aren't that much happier, let alone more kind? Yet we seem to be addicted to trying to shop our way into bliss.

But what if the government launched a public service campaign like its successful anti-smoking campaign to encourage the public to replace some of its buying of "stuff" with buying of services that hold greater promise of improving their quality of life. For example, hire a part-time: assistant to be:

- a helper to you in caring for your newborn
- a homework helper for your older child
- a personal assistant to do errands, laundry, wait for the repairperson, etc.
- a personal geek to teach you the technology you're afraid of

- a health care system advocate to help you get the care you need, affordably, in our labyrinthine, scary system
- a companion for your aging relative

Each of those jobs promise to significantly improve the life of the hirer and family. And the employee, piecing together a few such part-time jobs can make a reasonable living doing work that's unquestionably beneficial and ethical. Importantly, most of those jobs require only a modest skill set. Even many high school dropouts could likely find one such job they could do well enough.

How would hirers and employees match up? Just as they do for other jobs: hirers would place ads, for example, on Craigslist. If hirers want a professional to do the screening and payroll, they could turn to employment agencies. That would create yet more jobs.

To comment, click HERE[90].

17
JOB RETRAINING, REINVENTED

A *New York Times* review[91] of job retraining programs said: "For all the popularity of these government-financed programs, there are questions about whether they actually work."

But I'm wondering whether, rather than eliminating job training programs, what's required is a new approach to them.

Obviously, job training's effectiveness depends on who's doing the teaching. And training effectively isn't easy. Even courses at brand-name universities often don't generate great growth even in Ivy-caliber students. Think back to how few transformative instructors you had. And consider the frighteningly poor national freshman-to-senior growth[92]. It would be much more difficult still to recruit thousands of instructors capable of transforming the nation's long-term unemployed into the long-term well-employed -- in a new field, no less. After all, they'll have to compete with many other applicants who are or have been employed in that field and who don't have that huge resume gap that suggests they've been rejected by a number of employers.

Dream-Team-Taught Courses

An answer may be in what I call *dream-team-taught courses* taught online. Imagine if we asked a handful of the nation's proven most transformative instructors of the long-term unemployed to create and deliver an online job retraining course, say in communication skills. Then each of those instructors, paired with a computer programmer who specializes in interactive instruction, would create immersive, simulation-centric lessons. The resulting course would be made available free to all long-term unemployed people and perhaps to others.

That way all students, from Maine to California, Harlem to Beverly Hills, would -- instead of the usual mix of great, good, and bad instructors -- receive world-class job retraining at a fraction of the cost of live instructors. Some of the savings could be used to provide a live person at, for example, local unemployment offices, for the human touch.

What to teach

Of course, even with a dream-team of instructors, the course content must be right. And the content of most previous job retraining programs has been wrong. They've attempted to predict the fields likely to stay hot enough to justify telling the long-term unemployed: "Study this for six months or a year and you'll probably end up well-employed for a long time."

It's difficult to predict which fields will stay hot. For example, 10 years ago, we needed nurses, but by the time the next cohort of nurses were recruited and trained, hospitals had long since imported hordes of nurses, notably from the Philippines. A few years, we needed solar installers. Alas, the solar stock index[93], a forward-looking index of solar employment is down 95 percent(!) from its Dec. 2007 high, which, not coincidentally, when President Obama was first elected.

And even when the hot-job prognosticators picked right, too many trainees ended up unable to acquire the technical skills, or disliking or tiring of the job. Then, trained only in that narrow field, such people hadn't acquired skills that would transfer to another field.

So I believe that Job Training 2.0 should focus on training that wouldn't require a crystal ball on the job market nor on candidates' ability to succeed and be happy long-term in a particular career. It should provide training applicable to many fields. Two such topics that top my list:

Communication. Many people lose their jobs not for lack of technical chops but because they lack communication skills and/or are tone-deaf to office politics. Even top executives routinely hire coaches to learn the art of communication (okay, sometimes manipulation.) Some executives pay coaches as much as $250,000[94]! I'd bet that offering dream-team-taught online charm school would yield more employability and better employees than would field-specific training.

Shoestring Entrepreneurship. Even if the long-term unemployed graduated from a dream-team-taught charm school, in our challenging economy, I fear that too many of them wouldn't be able to convince employers to hire and retain them in a job paying middle income. Their best crack at higher income may be to learn how to be an entrepreneur.

I wouldn't train them for the high-risk entrepreneurship that MBA programs focus on: innovative, scalable, go-public companies. Instead, I'd teach the art of starting what I call a *shoestring business*: something that costs little to start, is ultrasimple, offers high profit margin, isn't offshoreable, and importantly, does not innovate, but rather replicates.

Why replicate? Because the leading edge too often turns out to be the bleeding edge--guinea pigs often die. And too few of the long-term unemployed can afford the failures so common among high-risk start-up ventures.

In a Shoestring Entrepreneurship course, I'd teach students how to start a, for example, shoeshine business:

1. Visit successful shoeshine stands. Amalgamate their best features into your shoeshine stand;

2. Secure a location with lots of well (ahem)-heeled foot traffic, for example, a major city's financial district;

3. Come up with a cute name for it, for example, Rise & Shine or Dianne Fineshine;

4. Run the business for a month to learn its ins and outs;

51

5. Set up a friend (perhaps another long-term unemployed person) in a second location, asking for a small percentage of the sales;

6. Keep cloning the business until you've made all the money you need.

To comment, click <u>HERE</u>[95].

18
THE WORKPLACE REINVENTED

If you're employed, you're probably asked to do more with less: harder, faster, better.

Why are employers so demanding?

There's no reason to believe that today's employers are crueler than past ones. What's different is that, in America, today's employers have crushing new costs that make it ever more difficult to stay in business: mountains of paperwork to comply with <u>federal</u>[96], state, and local regulations, more <u>employee lawsuits</u>[97], and government-required employer costs: from <u>worker's compensation</u>[98] to "non-worker's comp:" the <u>too-often abused</u>[99] Family and Medical Leave Act., and now ObamaCare.

And of course, employers are ever more subject to global competition. For example, in the not-so-distant past, U.S. car makers could get away with making inferior cars using parts with <u>deliberately short mean-time between failure/planned obsolescence</u>[100], and could afford to cave to the media-abetted unions and despite mediocre work, give assembly-line workers lifetime job guarantees and better compensation packages ($73 an hour) than most professionals receive. As a result, a large percentage of the price you paid for a car went to paying for inferior parts and for very expensive, not-great workers. Asian car companies such as Toyota and Honda offer <u>higher-quality-quality vehicles (average labor cost: $48 an hour</u>[101]) The U.S. keeps trying to prop up U.S carmakers: for example, a 25% tariff on foreign pickup trucks[102] and a taxpayer-funded $60 billion bailout of GM. Regarding the latter, despite statements by the Obama administration, <u>it has failed</u>[103]--the bailout occurred when the stock price was $34. The breakeven price is $53 but as of this writing is 20, a $16 billion loss for the taxpayer.

Yes, a small percentage of large American corporations are doing just fine and because their stock price is up, their executives make a fortune. But more broadly, because of the above factors, to survive, American employers, from auto makers to chip makers to small companies, and, yes even government agencies, must often ask workers to work harder, faster, better.

Alas, too many employees will crumble under the pressure. If you're lucky enough to have a job in this economy, you are ever more likely to get maxed out--you have no more blood to give.

So what's the answer? I believe the U.S. workplace can be reinvented so as to make worklife better for employees, while net, improving employers' products', services and bottom line.

Eight ideas for a better workplace

Of course, no one model will apply to all workplaces but I hope the eight ideas in this reinvention will at least stimulate your own thinking on how to improve your workplace.

1. No one-size-fits-all treatment of employees. Unions and gender/race advocacy groups often demand policies that require all employees be treated equally. Yet it's wiser to celebrate diversity: Each individual employee needs more or less supervision, more or less accountability, more or less flexibility of hours, more or less telecommuting, more or less of a workload. Employers deserve broader latitude in individualizing approaches to employees.

2. Convert at least some cubicles into *officettes*. The noise and lack of privacy in cubicles is draining. Employees' worklives would be more pleasant and employers would probably gain more in profitability if at least some cubes were converted into *officettes*: Use standard wallboard to raise the between-cubical screens to ceiling height, and add a door.

3. Expand telecommuting. With government having decided to try to force us out of our cars and into mass transit by not building freeways and thus increasing gridlock, commute times are growing. In many metropolitan areas, by the time we arrive at work, we've already used up a fair amount of our day's energy. Tack on the commute home and we're ever less likely to want to finish up any work nor have the energy to be a patient parent or domestic partner, let alone to do volunteer work. So, many employees spend most of their evening exhausted in front of a TV with a beer or something stronger.

53

Especially with the availability of free Skype video to augment phone and internet, more employees who feel they can be as or more productive working at home (or a Starbucks) should be allowed to do so, at least for part of the week. Not only would that reduce commute times, many employees are more relaxed at home, working in their comfies, with reduced child-care expenses. And the employer saves money by not needing to build or lease as much office space.

4. Allow pets. I'm aware that an inconsiderate pet owner could bring a fleabag to work. Solution: After one warning to use flea treatment, Fido's visitation rights could be revoked. Too, I'm aware that some people are allergic to or terrified of Fido. Solution: If Fido's owner's efforts to keep Fido away from Fearful fail or if Fearful's workspace can't be moved far enough from Fido, the doggie could be forced to turn in his employee badge.

The benefits of pets in the workplace outweigh the liabilities. According to a survey by the American Pet Products Manufacturers Association[104], most people believe that pets in the workplace make people happier, reduce stress, contribute to a more creative environment, and decrease absenteeism. That makes sense to me. Besides, think of how happy Fido will be to have its owner close at hand for a hug--and a much appreciated walk. Already, 17 percent of large companies allow pets at work[105]. More employers should.

5. Relax the dress code. Sure, some people love dressing up every day to go to work but many more find it time-consuming, expensive, and constraining. Personally speaking, I find a tie a mere step from a noose. And when I see someone (a lawyer, financial planner, etc) in a suit, I grab hold of my wallet--It makes me wonder if s/he didn't spend all that money on packaging himself to hide a lack of substance underneath. Dress codes should be more flexible. "Dress as you like" may sound extreme but, in most cases, I think that's wisest.

6. Improve the subtleties of workplace safety. Fortunately, the era of workplaces with toxic fumes and other noxiousness have largely been eradicated in the U.S. But more subtle yet still serious safety hazards exist. For example, millions of desks/workstations contribute to repetitive strain injuries such as carpal tunnel syndrome. Another example: research indicates that sitting too long can kill you[106]. A solution: an adjustable-height desk[107]. It allows you comfortably to, for example, work on a computer, while sitting or standing. Improving workspaces ergonomically is a cost-effective way to improve workers' lives.

7. Make ADA requirements more flexible. As with many laws, pressure groups have filed lawsuits forcing expansion of the Americans with Disabilities Act[108] well beyond the non-controversial improving wheelchair access, to everything from celiac disease[109] to chronic fatigue[110] so that now, for example, a person with a psychologist's note saying the employee is depressed is entitled to so-called "Reasonable Accommodation[111]."
On one hand, I understand the frustration of a person with a mental or physical illness or disability not wanting the additional burden of being persona non grata in the workplace. On the other hand, if employers are forced to assume the burden of employing such people, *net*, that causes harm:

- Coworkers often must take on extra work to "carry" the disabled employee,
- The shareholders who have invested their savings in the company lose money,
- All of us customers suffer from worse products or services.
- Employers that choose to terminate any of the 43 to 54 million Americans now covered under ADA bear the difficult burden of proving that the employee wasn't fired because of the disability. As a result, many employers retain poor performing employees, make Reasonable Accommodations for them, and accept the resulting reduced profitability and increased risk of going out of business. The companies are more at risk of going broke because, in every other country in the world ("the U.S. is a benchmark"[112],) employers are under less pressure to retain employees with serious mental or physical disabilities. And, of course, if a business goes bust, all its employees lose their jobs--devastating to their and their family's lives.

I believe that moderating the Americans with Disabilities Act would lead to greater net good while retaining fair treatment to all.

8. Make Affirmative Action policies more flexible. As with the ADA, no reasonable person could oppose Affirmative Action's original intent: to ensure that people of all races, religions, and sexual orientations are treated fairly.

But pressure from government and advocacy groups has converted the originally reasonable affirmative action laws and policies to, in practice, decreasing the weight of merit in hiring, promotion, and firing, and increasing the weight of non-merit-based criteria: aiming for proportionality in race, gender, age, and sexual orientation.

And government is now extending employment rights to the long-term unemployed and to ex-felons. For example, the Obama Administration has made it easier for ex-offenders to prevail in lawsuits by encouraging broader use[113] of such legal weapons as the Disparate Impact Theory of Discrimination. For example, in a biotechnology company, if there is a smaller percentage of African-Americans in leadership positions than in the general population, that is evidence of discrimination. **There's something Alice-in-Wonderland-like about pressuring employers to not give preference to applicants who haven't been felons nor been rejected by many other employers.**

Such policies are bad for coworkers, who thereby are forced to work with worse coworkers than would have been selected if hiring, promotion, and firing were based only on merit.

They're even bad for the protected classes: minorities, women, the disabled, sexual minorities. Too often, even fully qualified people in those classes are viewed askance: that they wouldn't have been hired if it weren't for their being, for example, an "underrepresented" minority.

Nor are such policies good for employers, whether companies, nonprofits, or government agencies. Their products and services are likely worse for feeling pressure to hire, promote, and fire, based on criteria other than merit. And such companies are more likely to fail, costing all the employees' jobs, because their competitors in other countries such as India and China are under less such pressure.

Of course, a few foolish employers will refuse to hire and promote the best candidates because of non-merit-based factors but, for the reasons cited, greater ill to society accrues from the massive "equal opportunity" enterprise. America would be wiser to reduce pressure to hire based on race, gender, sexual orientation, and age, let alone having been long-term unemployed or committed a felony.

Instead, American law and policy should simply encourage people perceiving discrimination to seek mediation, and, if that fails, arbitration, with taxpayer-funded subsidizing of legal fees for low-income claimants.

To comment, click HERE.[114]

19
CREATING MORE SUCCESSFUL, ETHICAL ENTREPRENEURS

Many of my clients aspire to self-employment, entrepreneurship. Much of what I teach them is the opposite of what's commonly taught in business school.

That's not surprising. I am critical of universities' attempts to prepare people for a career.

MIND OF AN
ENTREPRENEUR

For example, knowing that law schools, especially the prestigious ones, focus on theory not practice, good law firms have felt forced to create a practical training program for their new lawyers.

Indeed, many law professors don't know how to practice law. Anthony Kronman, when he was the Dean of Yale Law School, received a frantic call from a friend who had just been jailed: "Please, Tony, get me bailed out of here!" Kronman was forced to admit, "I don't know how."

Same is true of education. I have a Ph.D. from U.C. Berkeley specializing in the evaluation of innovation and, along the way, had to take courses from professors who taught in Berkeley's K-12 teacher-education program. They may have been assiduous researchers of arcana but as teachers, most were mediocre or worse. Certainly, none were the master K-12 teachers that should be training our teachers.

My physician says he learned most of how to be a good doctor after he finished medical school.

An Un-MBA

But it is in the field of business where I most closely observe how badly universities prepare people for their career. I have helped many of my clients to become successfully self-employed, and also have clients, colleagues, and friends with MBAs. **I see such discordance between the principles of starting and running a business taught in business school and what works in the real world:**

Business schools say "Innovate." That is very risky advice. Sure, a *large corporation* can take risks. Its deep pockets allow it to stay in business even if many attempts at innovations fail. But *individuals or small businesses* are likely to run out of money. Indeed, there are so many reasons why an innovation

57

might fail: development costs are high and subject to overruns, the product doesn't work, the public doesn't like it, the public too-quickly stops liking it, and/or a competitor comes up with a better or better-marketed product. That's why they say, "The leading edge often turns out to be the bleeding edge."

Sure it's fun to innovate and, sure, the world benefits from innovation but if you don't have the deep pockets to afford the multiple failures that precede even most successful entrepreneurs' success, it's wiser to replicate a successful type of business than to innovate.

It's easiest to find a successful business to replicate in small, therefore affordable retail: If a reasonable percentage of small retailers in a certain category are busy, it's a sign they're successful. So, for example, at lunchtime, there are lines in front of many food trucks. I'd simply watch the busy ones, incorporating their best practices plus recipes that got very high ratings on a respected internet recipe website. I'd hire the owner of one of those food trucks as a consultant to help me prepare to open-up shop. (I'd agree to not locate mine near his.) In sum, my mantra: **Don't innovate; replicate.**

If I did want to innovate, I can reduce my risk by asking deep-pocketed business owners and executives, "What in your business is annoying you?" If my queries yield a simple, doable business idea, I'd ask similar businesses if they have the same problem. If so, I'd have a reasonable basis for predicting that such a business that would have customers.

Biz schools urge you to quickly get big. "Scalable" is one of biz schools' favorite words. Alas, that too is dangerous advice for small businesses and especially for individuals wanting to be self-employed. True, even if the aforementioned food truck were successful, it probably wouldn't yield enough profit to earn me a sufficient living, so I would need to clone it in another good location. But I'd stop after just a few trucks--as soon as I netted $200,000 a year. The more locations, the less control you have over quality and cost control, and the difficulty of operating it well tends to mushroom. So I teach my clients, **"Don't be greedy. Get just big enough."** And live modestly so you'll always have enough money.

Biz schools focus on high-status businesses: high tech, biotech, medical devices, environmental technology, multinational corporations, etc. I teach my clients the opposite: start a low-status business, the lower the better. That way you're competing with less capable business owners. Few Stanford or Harvard graduates aspire to owning diesel repair shops, mobile home park cleaning services, installing and removing home-for-sale signs from lawns, shoeshine stands, cleaning out and installing cabinets in basements and garages, gourmet food trucks, rehabbing tenant-damaged apartment buildings, carts selling soup, scarves, knockoff designer purses, French soap, or coffee, or placing and maintaining laundry machines in apartment buildings. It's far easier to compete successfully in such low-status businesses. I teach my clients, **"Status is the enemy of success."**

Biz schools focus on intellectually meaty, complex businesses like the aforementioned high-tech, biotech, etc.. Alas, the more complex the business, the more that can go wrong. I teach my clients to choose a simple business, such as those I list in the previous paragraph. Each business location may yield insufficient profit to support a family but, once you've refined the concept, as I said, just clone your simple business in another location(s.) **Yes, keep it simple, stupid.**

Biz schools urge, "Choose a business with high barriers to entry;" that way it's tough for competitors to enter the market. That's valid advice if you're a deep-pocketed corporation but it's usually dead wrong if you're the typical cash-strapped entrepreneur. I recommend that most aspiring entrepreneurs start a business that requires little capital and then, as mentioned, use its profits to clone it.

Biz schools assert, "It takes money to make money." I teach the opposite: You must constantly look for ways to get what you need for little or no money. For example, I urge that, where possible, you run your business out of your home, car, a Starbucks, a condo development's community room, or friend's apartment that's vacant during the day. When buying something, I urge such cost-effectiveness techniques as to ask yourself, "What must this cost to manufacture?" That enabled, for example, one of my clients to buy silk scarves wholesale for $1 a piece than from another wholesaler who wanted $10. Of course, I also encourage my clients to consider buying last year's model, used or cosmetically flawed items, and using the Internet for price shopping. In short, I teach my clients, **"Start with 'How can I, without undue hassle, get this for free or very cheaply?'"**

Biz schools urge entrepreneurs to delegate: "You can't do everything," they urge. In contrast, I encourage my clients to, when starting their business, to do as much as possible themselves. Of course, that conserves cash--the life blood you must preserve lest you go out of business before you become profitable. Also, spending time immersed in the business's weeds tends to build your psychological ownership in and enthusiasm for the business. Most important, being hands-on allows you to gain deep understanding of how to make the business work.

For example, if my goal were to make $200,000 a year from a chain of shoeshine stands, I'd run the first one myself, taking full shifts doing the shoeshines. That would enable me to truly understand the customers, the art of shoe shining, identify upsell opportunities, how to optimize the experience for the shoe shiner and the customer, theft and vandalism problems, disgruntled customer issues, everything. Only when I really knew the business and it was clearly becoming successful would I clone it and *then* delegate by hiring someone to run the two shoeshine stands. I would take all the time needed to find great employees and would treat them well, for ethical reasons and because I want them loyal to me. Even then, I would remain actively involved in the business: visiting, training, inspiring, and, where needed, setting limits. My rule: **Don't delegate prematurely or too much.**

An Un-MBA Way to Start a Business

As a way of summarizing, here's how I'd start the aforementioned shoeshine business to maximize my chance of ethically and relatively quickly, netting $200,000 a year:

1. I'd search Google and Amazon to find the best articles and books on running a shoeshine business.

2. Using service review sites such as Yelp, I'd identify a half-dozen shoeshine stands that had excellent reviews and many reviews. The latter would indicate that a business has many customers.

3. I'd visit each of those shoeshine stands and note everything: the characteristics of the location, signage, menu and prices, equipment, products used, procedure used, ergonomics, the shiner/customer interactions, how people who needed to wait were dealt with, amenities, everything. I'd buy a shoeshine at each stand and while getting the shine, ask such questions as, "What should I know about running a shoeshine business that might surprise me?"

4. I'd amalgamate into my shoeshine stand the best practices in the articles and books I've read and the half-dozen shoeshine stands I visited.

5. I would take the time to find an excellent location that I could get for free. (Remember, my rule: "Start with free.") For example, I'd ask the owner or manager of a large office building to let me run my stand for free in the lobby. My pitch: "That enables you to provide a useful service for your tenants without it costing you a dime."

6. I'd run the shoeshine stand myself for a week, a month, whatever it took for me to fully understood the business.

7. Then, because I don't want to make a career of shining people's shoes, I'd take all the time needed to find an excellent person to replace me.

8. Next, I'd turn my attention to finding another excellent location and an excellent person to staff it. I'd keep expanding only until I netted $200,000 a year, always staying actively involved to ensure the quality remained high, my shoeshiners happy, and my profit adequate.

9. Finally, I'd sell the business or keep it as a cash cow while I turned to my next project: entrepreneurial, social entrepreneurial, or volunteer.

To comment, click <u>HERE</u>[115].

20
DO WHAT YOU LOVE AND STARVE?

So many Americans try to follow their passion and end up waiting tables. That's a waste for them and for the country. They could do so much more.

If you are a star—brilliant, talented, motivated, personable, low-maintenance--and you have a passion, even if it's in a competitive field, sure, go for it.

This reinvention is for everyone else.

Based on the 4,000 clients I've worked with in the last 25 years, the hundreds of callers to my career-centric radio show, and my countless other conversations with people about their careers, I've come to the conclusion that we've been sold a bill of goods when we're told to "Follow your passion, " or "Do what you love and the money will follow." Fact is, if you do what you love, you well may starve.

Yes, some people do what they love and the money follows but millions have followed their passion and still haven't earned enough to even pay

back their student loans, let alone make even a bare middle-class living doing what they love.

The problem with "Do what you love!"

The problem is that too many people crave the same few careers, for example, the arts, environmental, and non-profit work. Employers in such fields get dozens if not hundreds of applications for each middle-income-paying job. So to get the job., you have to be a star or extremely well connected

In other cases, salaries tend to be minimal or non-existent. Do what you love and volunteer work well may follow.

The irony is that the small percentage of people who do make a living in "do-what-you-love," "follow-your-passion" careers, are, on average, no happier than people in less sexy jobs. Here's why. Plenty of "cool careers" sound better than they turn out to be. Actors, for example, spend very little time acting. They spend most of their time auditioning, licking their wounds when they don't get cast, or if they do get cast, sitting around waiting for their turn at rehearsals or on movie or commercial shoots.

More important, not only do salaries in "cool" careers tend to be low, employers in those fields know they can get away with treating employees shabbily because zillions of other capable people are panting for the chance to work 60 hours a week for $27,521 (with no benefits) rarely getting praise in exchange for the good feeling of knowing they're playing an infinitesimal role in saving the spotted owl or whatever, even though they may never get closer to an owl than to a pile of accounts receivable statements.

Other people's passion is status. So, for example, they endure years of difficult and/or boring law school and accumulate boatloads of student debt for the privilege of slaving under a 2,000-billable-hour quota for the law firm of Dewey, Cheatham, and Howe, with a futon in their office so they can sneak in a few zzzzs in the middle of the all-nighters they pull to boost the chances of their corporate client getting money from the opposing lawyer's corporate client.

Other status seekers prostitute themselves to climb the corporate ladder. They work 60+-hour workweeks and kiss up to their bosses, smilingly willing to uproot themselves and their families for a few years in whatever God-forsaken place The Company wants to dump them. They endure two years of impractical arcana and take on a mountain of debt in graduate school so they can put those three letters, M, B, and A on their resume. And for what? So they may finally get a title of director or vice president, and after their 12-hour, cover-their-butt workday, be one of the many execs who collapse on their sofa, get blitzed, and stare at their oversized living room in their oversized neighborhood wondering, "Is that all there is?"

In contrast, if your job is mundane, for example, marketing coordinator for Walla Walla Widget Works, the employer knows there aren't hundreds of competent people champing at the bit for your job. So to keep you, the employer is more likely to offer decent working conditions, reasonable work hours, kind treatment, opportunities for learning, and pay you well. Those are the things that—much more than being in a "cool" career-- are likely to lead to career contentment.

You say you want status? Unless you're a true star (brilliant, driven, great personality, or have great connections), you may want to give it up. As I said earlier, **status is the enemy of success.** You're more likely to find career contentment in a not-high-status career. In my mind, someone who's an honorable assistant at Walla Walla Widget Works. is more worthy of respect than are many lawyers, salespeople, and business development VPs I know. If someone thinks less of you because you're job isn't high-status, they don't deserve to be your friend.

Advice I'd Give My Child
If you're at all entrepreneurial, I recommend starting your own business. Yes, I know, only 20 percent of new businesses are still in business after five years, but you can beat the odds. Just remember this rule: **Don't innovate. Replicate.** Copy a successful simple business. Innovations are too risky: Your product might not work, may not be popular with the public, or a competitor could beat you to market. Why be a guinea pig? Unless you have deep pockets or are truly brilliant, the risks are too great. Many people have ended up in poverty because of their innovations. Even Tivo, a wonderful product, lost hundreds of millions of dollars in the first few years. Last I checked, you don't have oodles of money to lose. Leave the innovations to corporations or the independently wealthy.

Where to find a business to copy? Drive around to find a simple business at which customers are lined up out the door. For example, see a successful burrito shop or espresso cart? Open a similar one in a similar neighborhood. Hire your friends to staff it. Your chances of success will be much higher than that 20 percent. You will find happiness in providing an in-demand product at a fair price. Confine your urge to innovate to your hobbies.

Another approach to finding a good business is to pick a grungy one, for example, automatic transmission repair or mobile home park maintenance. Few top-notch people go into such businesses, so if you do it competently, you'll have little competition and probably make good maybe great money. And you'll feel better about your work, having people coming to you and thanking you, and owning your own business rather than slaving away for some boss ever fearing your job will be consolidated, automated, or shipped to India.

You say you don't have the knowledge to run such a business? No problem. For example, I don't know a thing about transmissions, but if I wanted to open a transmission shop, I'd find the best transmission mechanic, pay him well and hire a consultant who is the owner of a successful transmission shop located far enough from my store that he wouldn't fear my competition. The two of them would teach me how to set up my business. Then, I'd spend my time building relationships with car repair shop owners so I'd get their referral business.

If you're not entrepreneurial and want to be well employed, go far from the madding crowd. Here are some areas where the job market is not hypercompetitive: Court reporting, car finance & insurance, accounting, insurance, sales of little known commercial products, health care administration, fundraising, financial services, anything serving Latinos (entertainment, schools, hospitals, criminal justice system), anti-terrorism, and biotech regulatory affairs.

Remember that, in the end, the key to career contentment is a job that:
--isn't too hard or too easy
-- has a boss who's kind and helpful
-- involves an ethical product or service
--requires a reasonable commute
-- pays reasonable well and offers benefits
-- doesn't require 70-hour work weeks
-- offers opportunities to learn and grow.

You're more likely to find these things and, in turn, career contentment by pursuing an unpopular career than the millions pursuing a "cool" one.

To comment, click HERE[116].

21

THE ONE-WEEK JOB SEARCH

It takes the average person a half year to land a job, a year if you're 55+. What a mammoth waste of a person's and the nation's resources. The following job-search method would get job seekers matched with the right employer in much less time. That would benefit both the job seeker and the nation's employers.

I'm not saying the *one-week job search* will be an easy week. Indeed, it will take longer than a week if you're trying to find a job while working full-time. But that short-term effort should be worth it, certainly better so than the drips-and-drabs job search most people undertake and ever-more give up on:

- You'll have completed most of a job search's yucky tasks in just a week or so.
- Having made all your contacts in a short time, you've maximized your chances of getting more than one job offer at around the same time. Having that choice of job offers allows you to pick the one with the best combination of good boss, good work, good learning opportunities, and reasonable compensation. Because of that, my clients find that the one-week job search is more likely to lead to career contentment than pursuing a so-called cool career.

MONDAY

Write your resume. Use Microsoft Word's resume templates or *ResumeMaker* software to create or revise your resume. Incorporate into your resume, two or three brief PAR stories. a **P**roblem you faced, the impressive way you **A**pproached it, and its positive **R**esolution. Also see if you can incorporate praise quotes from bosses, peers, supervisees, or customers.

Get feedback on a draft, ideally from people you know in your target field. Post it on LinkedIn, not naming your current employer if you don't want your employer to know you're looking.

Craft a 5-second, 10-second and 30-second pitch. Each one must explain why you're looking for a job, what you're looking for, and proof you're good. For example, a five-second pitch might be: "The company downsized so I'm looking for another CPA position. I never thought I'd be looking for a job—I have always gotten good evaluations, but that's the way it goes." The 30-second pitch adds information about the kind of job you're looking for and/or provides credible evidence that you bring a lot to the table. You will

65

often want to modify your pitch so it impresses the particular person you're talking to.

Have a ready answer for the question(s) you're most afraid you'll be asked, for example, "Why have you job-hopped so much?" or "If you're so good, how come you've been unemployed for a year?"

TUESDAY

Identify 25 employers you'd like to work for, without regard to whether they're currently advertising any openings. Most job seekers should focus on growing organizations in their target field within reasonable commuting distance. How to find them? One approach is to zip-code search the millions of job openings aggregated on indeed.com, simplyhired.com and linkedin.com to find companies with multiple job openings. Government jobs are rarely advertised except on their own websites. To find federal agencies with openings, go to **www.usajobs.opm.gov**. To find state jobs in all 50 states: http://50statejobs.com/gov.html. For more sources of job leads: http://bit.ly/xcsEPm.

Research the 25 employers. Take just a few minutes on each. Simply look at the organization's website and Google the employer's name. Have a file in which you store notes about each employer. Note: In some fields, much hiring is done by agencies, for example, in accounting, the Robert Half Agency. If so, add those agencies to your list of potential employers.

If you are looking for a job for which you are unusually well qualified, also add headhunters to your list of contacts. Find the right ones by calling a human resources department of a large company and ask which headhunter they use to fill the sort of position you're seeking.

Contact the 25 people in your network most likely to help you get a job, especially a job at one of your 25 target employers. Use email, phone, or set up an in-person meeting, whichever you think would be best with that person. Give your 5-, 10- or 30-second pitch and then ask, "Might you know someone at any of these 25 employers, or elsewhere for that matter, who you think I should talk with?" If not, ask, "Would you keep your ears open for me, and if I'm still looking in a month, would you mind if I followed up with you?" If appropriate, also ask if your contact would review your resume and cover letter or do a mock interview with you.

WEDNESDAY

Email or phone any leads given to you by your network that are *not* among the 25 employers you've targeted.

Try to contact the person who would be your boss, but an HR person is okay too. Pleasant persistence can, *often enough*, get you through. Voice mail is fine.

Start with your 10-second pitch, enthusiastically delivered. (Smile when talking on the phone.) If you're talking to a person, not voice mail, listen more than talk. Ask questions about the employer's needs so you can better understand how you might be helpful. If you have an idea, propose it, but tactfully, for example, "In listening to you, I'm wondering if I could help you by doing X. What do you think?" If you think it would impress that employer, tell one or two of your PAR stories.

Visit each of the 25 employers' websites and apply for any on-target jobs. Start your cover letter by mentioning your referrer, if any. Then explain, point-by-point, how you meet the requirements stated in the ad. Include a sentence or two that capitalizes on the knowledge you obtained yesterday about that employer.

Your goal is, by the end of the week, to have applied for five openly advertised on-target jobs. You probably won't find five on those 25 employers' sites. Find the rest on employment websites. For a good list, see www.rileyguide.com/jobs.html.

THURSDAY AND FRIDAY (and Saturday, if needed)
On those 25 employers' websites, if there is no listed job to apply for, write a brief email to a senior employee, ideally one with the power to hire you. Example: "I'm a good operations manager who's just been part of a downsizing at the BigWhup Widget Corp. *(Insert something about you that would impress that employer.)* I'm attracted to your company because I have experience in your industry, liked what I saw on your website *(insert a specific),* and, I must admit, because I live just ten minutes away. I'm attaching my resume. I'd welcome the opportunity to speak with you or a designee to see if and how I might be of help to you.
Sincerely,
Joe Jobseeker

Also, finish and send those five job applications you identified on Wednesday.

If, within a week, you haven't heard from people you've contacted, call to follow up. Don't hesitate to leave voice mail. If, for example, you had cold-contacted an employer, say something like, "I'm *(insert your name)*, the manager at the BigWhup Widget Company who was just part of a downsizing and phoned you. I'm assuming that not having heard from you, you're not interested. But I know that sometimes, things can fall between the cracks, so I'm taking the liberty of calling to follow up. If you or a colleague would be willing to speak with me, if only to offer advice where I might turn, I'd welcome a call. My phone number is *(repeat the number twice.)* My name, again, is *(insert name.)* Thank you."

Of course, you'll not hear back from most of the people you contact—even from the employers whose ads you're responding to--but you will likely get sufficient bites. Often it's from an employer who has been thinking about hiring but hasn't gotten to the laborious process yet. Sometimes, an employer finds it easier to just vet you and be done with it.

If the above method doesn't bear fruit, repeat the process with a different job or industry target and/or seek assistance from a private career counselor or government-sponsored OneStop. (To find your local OneStop, go to www.servicelocator.org.)

To comment, click HERE[117].

22
GAINING WILLPOWER

So many people can't motivate themselves to do what they know they should. If we could grow in willpower and reduce procrastination, not only would we feel better about ourselves and be more productive, the U.S. would be a more viable competitor in the global economy.

Having been career coach to 4,000 people, I've so often had to help people improve their willpower. Here are the twelve strategies that have been most helpful to the most people. Might one or more help you?

1. Embrace work. Work can feel as or more rewarding than play. Even though I enjoy, for example, watching movies, I actually feel better about, for example, writing this book. Because my work isn't too hard or too easy, it is pleasurable, and I feel I'm making a contribution, unlike when I'm watching a movie.

Work was a wonderful healer for my dad. After surviving the Holocaust, he was dumped from a cargo ship into the Bronx. He took the first job he could find--sewing shirts in a Harlem factory. It distracted him from his past and gave him hope for a better future. He finally saved up enough to open a tiny retail store in a bad neighborhood. While he didn't love his work, it kept him from living in the past and made him feel purposeful, providing a decent life for his wife, my sister, and me.

It may be easier to embrace work if you always ask yourself, "What's the fun way to do this?" Even job searching can be reframed to be more fun. View resume-writing as a way to figure out all the good things about yourself. Think of cold-calling as a treasure hunt, a videogame in which you encounter monsters and fairy godmothers, a backdoor into a crowded employment front door. Think of a job interview not as an interrogation but as a first date, in which you're both trying to figure out if you should become more involved.

2. If possible: set an exciting goal. Goethe said, "Small dreams motivate no one." Worried about the risk of a trying for a big goal? You can usually control the risk. For example, use the time-honored approach of having a stable mundane job to fund your ability to pursue your dream. For example, Wallace Stegner waited tables at night and wrote during the day. He ended up winning a Pulitzer for his writing and founded Stanford's creative writing program, where his students included Sandra Day O' Connor, Ken Kesey, and Larry McMurtry. Remember too that even if you don't achieve your goal--for example, you never get published--your life is richer for having tried, and you didn't, in the process, risk destitution.

3. Tell your goal to your loved ones--To avoid the embarrassment of admitting to your loved ones that you procrastinated, you may be more motivated to complete the task.

4. List the reasons you're hesitating to act. Then write what your wisest self would say to counter or sidestep each. Stuck? Ask a trusted friend.

5. Don't think; act. Psychologist William James wrote, "The more we struggle and debate, the more we reconsider and delay, the less likely we are to act." Don't wait until you feel better before you act. It's the opposite: act and you will feel better.

6. Here is the six-step procrastination cure I teach my clients:

1. Decide if the task is worth doing: Picture the benefits. Picture the downside. If it is worth doing, do you *love yourself* enough to delay the short-term pleasure of avoiding the task for the long-term rewards that come from accomplishing it?

2. Be aware of *The Moment of Truth*: the moment you decide whether or not to start the task. Being conscious of that moment makes you more likely to choose to do it.

3. Break the task down to baby steps. Don't know how? Get help.

4. Keep repeating this mantra: It needn't be perfect. It needn't be fun. It just need be done.

4. Overwhelmed by the task? Try asking yourself, "What's my next one-second task?" Do that a few times and you may have jump-started yourself.

5. Be aware of your crisis points: when you're likely to screw up, for example, the moment before you start eating.

6. *The One-Minute Struggle*: After a minute of struggle, you're unlikely to make more progress. Instead, you are likely to get frustrated and quit the task. So after a minute, get help or see if you can do the task without doing that hard part.

7. Make it a ritual. For example, if you're a job seeker, every day, be at your desk at say 9 am, take a five-minute break at 9:25, back for another 25 minutes, then another five-minute break and so on.

8. Keep your goal top-of-mind--It's easy to forget that you need to work on that project. Use Memotome.com or Google Calendar to send you frequent emails reminding you. I'm trying to lose 10 pounds, so twice a day, I get an email that says, "Reasons to lose weight: live longer, clothes fit, look better. And remember, 'a moment on the lips; a lifetime on the hips.'" **It's important that you repeatedly read aloud that message, perhaps three times a day. Otherwise, it won't penetrate into your brain's neurons.**

9. Use Stickk.com. You commit to a goal and if you don't achieve it, you automatically make a donation to a charity you don't like. For example, if you're pro-choice, the donation goes to a pro-life organization.

10. Go all the way: Instead of tackling your task in drips and drabs, totally immerse yourself in it. When it was time for me to start writing my first book, I moved out of my house for a week. I rented a cabin on the ocean, just took my laptop and my portable keyboard for recreation, and wrote for eight hours a day for a week. I got so into writing the book that it was easy for me to continue writing when I got home.

Another example of my going all the way: The only time I lost weight was when I was on a strict diet in which every day, I ate the same foods adding up to 1,200 calories a day. That took the choice out of the matter.

11. Try affirmations. Some experts believe that repeating positive affirmations, for example, "I am going to do this!," and visualizing your succeeding, changes your brain's neuronal structure, leading to more positive behavior. Sports psychologists use visualization with pro athletes.

Viktor Frankl claims that positive thinking helped him survive the Holocaust.

12. Have a cheerleader or slave driver cheering, jeering, and/or guilt-tripping you into action.

Don't let setbacks stop you prematurely. When you have one, remember that most successful people have suffered many setbacks. But winners don't get depressed about it--They try to learn from the setback and move on. Of course, if you fail and fail and fail again at something, perhaps the world is telling you that you need a different goal. As Kenny Rogers says, "You gotta know when to hold 'em, know when to fold 'em.

To comment, click HERE.[118]

23
CAREER COUNSELING REINVENTED

Key to a society's thriving is its citizens finding careers, jobs, and self-employment for which they are well-suited and then developing the skills to be successful in their work. In theory, career counselors should be crucial facilitators of that but usually they're not.

Career Counselor

Why career counselors fail

Career counselors try to help their clients find a career that matches their skills, interests, values, and personality. But too often they come up with

- too few or too many career possibilities
- an ostensibly good-fit career that turned out not to be
- an ostensibly poor-fit career that worked out fine
- a long-shot career: Someone who likes performing wants to be a movie star. Good luck.

In technical terms, the predictive validity of career assessments, even when combined with counselor subjective judgment, is poor.

Nor are career counselors inordinately successful in helping clients find good employment. To help people land a job, career counselors guide (or too often write) resumes, cover letters, and urge networking and cold contacting employers. Those strategies too often fail because the pool of people who seek out a career counselor disproportionately don't have top-of-the-stack backgrounds, have weak networks, are lousy networkers and/or are too shy or not-quick-on-their-feet enough to successfully cold-contact employers.

Even when career counselors succeed in helping their client land a position, they, net, make society *worse*! In a tight job market, it's a zero-sum game: If a career counselor helps a client land a job for which he or she would not be the best candidate, a better candidate loses out just because s/he couldn't afford to hire a career counselor to package him and optimize his interview presence--from demeanor to pitch to parrying questions such as, "Why have you been unemployed so long?" Not only does that career counselor thereby saddle employers and the coworkers with weak employees, that worsens the employer's product or service, thus hurting society.

Career counselors are especially unethical when they help weak candidates with their resume. In deciding whom to interview, employers are wise to use resumes not just to look at their reported work history but to compare candidates' ability to think, organize, and clearly present information, Those are key to so many jobs. So when someone uses someone else to write or even edit their resume, it's of course, unfair to candidates that wrote their own resume because they recognize it's the ethical thing to do and/or because they couldn't afford to hire a resume writer. A resume writer also is unfair to the employer, who used the misleading resume as part of the hiring decision, thus likely saddling the employer with a worse employee than would otherwise have been hired. A resume writer also is unfair to the coworkers on that job, who are forced to work with a worse person than if a resume writer hadn't committed the subterfuge. And ultimately, a resume writer is unfair to society, because when the best candidates are not hired, we all get worse products and services.

If hiring a professional to write or even edit a resume were ethical, why do resume writers never credit their work on their clients' resumes?

Thus the field of career counseling is ripe for reinvention.

Career counseling reinvented

Here are things career counselors could do that would yield a far higher success rate while being completely ethical and abetting society:

- Because it's so difficult for the typical person who consults a career counselor to change to a more rewarding career, especially in today's tough job market, career counselors are mostly likely to be of greatest benefit in helping people, not in landing a job, but in becoming more successful on their current job or preparing them for greater success on their next job or self-employment.

  Examples: Helping them renegotiate their job description to match their strengths, identifying and coaching them in their areas for growth, for example, communication, handling conflict, running meetings, time management, stress management, anger management, attitude improvement, mentoring supervisees, managing upward, starting a business, helping overcome procrastination, etc.

- The matching of a person's attributes with careers is much abetted by software such as www.CareerInfoNet.org. In addition to helping a person find well-suited careers, CareerInfoNet often provides videos of what the job is like, lists places to get trained, even how to finance your training.
- Career counselors should help clients land only jobs for which they are well-qualified.
- Career counselors should be paid for performance, for example, if the client lands the six-figure job he's seeking. That would result in career counselors accepting only clients they believe they can succeed with. That would also incent the counselor to work quickly rather than be paid more with ever additional session.

- Career counselors should teach job seekers how to use the internet to find truly well-suited job openings and then use a *point-by-point cover letter* to demonstrate that good fit: List each job requirement in the job ad and briefly explain you meet the requirement. Note that this is ethically solid: the counselor is simply helping to match an employee with an appropriate employer. That stands in contrast to the aforementioned career counselors who write people's resumes and cover letters and do interview coaching, which often make a prospect look better than s/he really is.

- Because so many people are having a hard time landing a decent job, career counselors should offer clients low-risk/high-payoff self-employment ideas and tactics. The problem is that many career counselors are not great businesspeople so they may not be the best teachers of entrepreneurship.

To comment, click HERE[119].

24
THE METER: A SIMPLE WAY TO MAKE US MORE PRODUCTIVE

Many people believe that The Goal is happiness. I disagree.

Focusing on happiness trivializes life's meaning. You could fill your life with activities that make you happy: sex, favorite foods, movies, a Lexus, a beautiful house, I'll even throw in a front-row seat at a Lady Gaga concert. Yet you would die leaving the world no better for your presence. And the extent to which you have left the world better is, in my view, the most valid criterion for assessing whether you've lived a worthwhile life.

It helps us to live that life well-led if we use *The Meter*: -10 (selling crack to kids) to +10 (working to cure cancer) every time we're deciding what to do next. We simply ask ourselves, "What could I do that would score high on The Meter?"

On a recent radio show, I discussed that approach to the life well-led with a leading public intellectual, Richard Posner[120]. He raised objections:

- **It's too joyless.** I stipulated to that but argued, as above, that making the world better is more important than an individual's pleasure.
- **Most people aren't willing or able to subordinate happiness to productivity,** even if, in the abstract, they believe that's wise. My response: the perfect is the enemy of the good. As with most philosophies and religious principles, they are ideals to which to aspire. Because we are human, we will never achieve perfection but better for even a few additional people to strive toward an admirable benchmark than for them to live the life unexamined or in the service of less worthy goals.
- **Most people can't make enough of a difference** to make it worth sacrificing pleasure. I disagreed. Take, for example, an accounts-payable clerk deciding on Saturday whether to watch a football game or to pay the bills he couldn't finish paying on Friday. If he chooses to pay those bills, he ensures the recipients have their money to spend when they're supposed to have it. If instead, the clerk elects to watch the football game, the recipient suffers unfairly. So even in this example of a relatively low-impact person, his selecting the activity that would score higher on The Meter makes a significant difference. Multiply that by the clerk's countless such decisions and by all the people who might choose to use The Meter, and the total benefit is large.
- **The lack of recreation would hurt their health** thereby, net, resulting in their doing less good for the world. In fact, working at what one does well is usually less stressful than are many recreational activities. For example, many sports game watchers' and video game players' blood pressure likely rise more than when doing pro-social work.

Even a lauded activity such as caring for one's child is often more stressful and less beneficial than more pro-social work. Spending an hour fighting with your kids to clean their room or do their homework is stressful, and the research is getting ever clearer that parenting has far smaller impact on a child's development than is commonly believed. A more likely to be societally beneficial hour would be such seemingly less important tasks as ensuring even that bills are paid, let alone if it's a cardiologist seeing an extra patient at the end of the day a policymaker taking an extra hour to optimize consumer-protection legislation, or a cancer researcher deciding to try another research avenue rather than to play Monopoly with his kids.

Let's say you accept my definition of the life well-led: spending as much of life as possible making the biggest difference possible. If so, key to accomplishing that is simply to keep The Meter top-of-mind: Every time you're deciding how to spend the next chunk of time, ask yourself, "What would that score on The Meter?"

I believe that encouraging the public to use The Meter in guiding their life would do much to, not only make their lives more meaningful, but to improve America.

To comment, click HERE[121].

REINVENTIONS OF EDUCATION

25
TOWARD EDUCATION LIVING UP TO ITS PROMISE

Education is widely viewed as our best hope: for competing in the global economy, for reducing the racial and socio-economic achievement gap, and for all of us to live up to our potential. Alas, the data is clear that education has heretofore been more of an aspirin than a magic pill.

And the problem doesn't appear to be lack of spending. Some readers may be surprised to learn that for decades, the **U.S. ranks #1 or #2 in per capita spending on education yet, <u>in the most recent international comparison</u>[122] of education outcomes, America now ranks 23rd, tied with Poland, while Shanghai is #1.**

And despite disproportionate spending on compensatory education for a half century now, the racial and socioeconomic achievement gap remains as wide as ever. Perhaps most dispiriting is the research on Head Start, which had long been seen as the best hope for reducing the achievement gap. **In 2010, <u>the definitive evaluation</u>[123] of four decades of research on Head Start was published. It finds the same as have nearly all previous studies: Head Start yields no significant, enduring positive effects.**

What is typically proposed for improving education has yielded poor results in trials, for example, reduced class size and increased expectations. The following ideas would seem to have a better chance of making education the magic pill we wish it were.

Dream-Team-Taught Courses taught on video

As mentioned earlier in the reinvention of job retraining, imagine that every student--rich and poor, urban and rural--would be taught by a dream team of the world's most effective, inspirational teachers. If anything could be expected to increase education's potency, it would seem to be that. Each class session, presented on video and viewable on the Internet, would consist of the teachers' presentations abetted by world-class visuals, immersive demonstrations, etc. A live teacher or paraprofessional would be on-site to provide the human touch: answer questions, be encouraging, keep kids focused, etc. Alternatively, those dream-team-taught online lecturettes could replace the often blown-off homework.

A first-things-first curriculum

In the abstract, most people would agree that it's better that students graduate high school able to analyze a newspaper's editorial even if they don't understand Shakespeare's allusions, that they think probabilistically even if they can't solve simultaneous equations, that they fully understanding the scientific method even if they can't manipulate chemical reactions. Even more would agree that it would be wrong that interpersonal communication, parenting, and financial literacy be nearly absent from the curriculum.

Yet in the real world, our curriculum demands the opposite. Indeed, don't many of us know people with even advanced degrees who lack the ability to handle life's basics? **Defenders of our arcana-first curriculum argue that practical matters should be taught at home. That's a nice ideal but far from realistic. Schools should first teach what's most important so that, by graduation, students have learned what's most important for living.**

Reinvigorate programs for high-potential students

After Sputnik, fearful of Soviet domination, America wisely invested more resources in educating our "best and brightest." But over the last half-century, the U.S. has moved to prioritizing education for low achievers. Egalitarianism and redistributive "justice" are trumping investing in kids with higher potential. Especially below the high school level, classes and schools for high-ability/"gifted" kids have, in many locales, largely been dismantled.

But for America to thrive in our ever more competitive global economy as well as to ensure the flow of great discoveries, great leaders, etc., it's time for renewed attention to the now too-ignored, high-ability child. Just as there are special education classes for low-achievers, there should be special classes and schools and summer programs for brilliant kids, even those who are not high achievers in school. Some of our smartest kids eschew (wisely?) much of the required school curriculum but when motivated, can do amazing things. And if given a chance, they can learn the curriculum in a fraction of the standard time. For example, at the Center for Talented Youth, high-ability kids complete year-long high school courses in just three weeks[124].

Mentorship

Most transformational change occurs not in a classroom, but one-on-one. Educators should take a lesson from online dating services such as match.com and provide a mentor/protégé matching service online. This could be peer-mentoring or adult-to-child mentoring and could be done locally or, like match.com, nationally, in which case mentoring would occur by phone, email, and Skype. Such remote mentoring offers the advantage of minimizing the potential for mentors abusing their protégés.

High-quality college-prep <u>and</u> direct-to-career paths

One of education's ironies is that diversity is a core principle, yet ever more of its leaders insist on one-size-fits-all education. Today's mantra is "College for all!"

But let's step back and look at that dispassionately. Imagine that after nine years of school (K-8,) like millions of students, you were still struggling with sixth-grade-level reading and math. Now you're starting the 9th grade and required to do four more years of ever more difficult academic work: While you're still trying to figure out long division, you're asked to solve quadratic equations. While you're still struggling with that fifth-grade level reading book, you're asked to write essays explaining the themes and symbolism in Silas Marner. Unless you are an unusually "good" (compliant) kid, mightn't you become dispirited, feel hopeless, and view your ever worsening grades as a sign that society deems you a failure, a loser, and so you give up, drop out and feel you have little to lose by abusing drugs, joining a gang, and/or getting pregnant?

People are often called elitist or even racist dare they assert that some students would be wiser to select a direct-to-career high school curriculum instead of a college-preparatory one. In such a curriculum, students would improve their reading, math, etc., not with classic literature, history, algebra, and foreign-language textbooks, but while preparing for a career they could enter directly after high school, for example, a robotics technician, chef, or entrepreneur.

The irony is that those calling for a one-size-fits-all education are the ones who are being elitist. They believe that, for all people, white-collar jobs are intrinsically better than blue-collar jobs and so, even if a student's abilities and limitations suggest that a blue-collar direction is a better fit, that student should be forced onto a white-collar path to--in another irony--"to keep their options open."

But fact is, such students usually find the path to and through college less beneficial than a direct-to-career path would have been. Even if a student who was reading on a sixth-grade level in the ninth grade takes a college preparatory curriculum and manages to graduate (often the result of grade inflation) and even if that student went on to college, and even if that student defied the 3:1 odds against such students earning their bachelor's degree even if given 8 1/2 years[125], they're likely to be less employable than if they had pursued a direct-to-career path. Today, even strong college graduates are struggling to land white-collar jobs while skilled blue-collar jobs go wanting.

Others object that a direct-to-career program can become a dumping ground: poorly staffed and funded. They needn't be. Such programs can and should be of as high quality as a college-preparatory program, as they are in other countries[126], for example, Japan, Germany, and in Scandinavia.

It seems obvious that students should have a choice and not be forced into a one-size-fits-all education. Many teachers agree. But educrats and politicians get more votes with such superficially appealing slogans as, "High standards for all students! "No soft bigotry of low expectations!" Such slogans have apple-pie appeal but in practice, ruin countless lives. A wiser slogan would be "I'm pro-choice in education."

Finding transformational college instructors

I've been listening to courses on CD from the Teaching Company. Those courses are taught by renowned teaching-award-winning professors yet I've been disappointed.

The Teaching Company, indeed most students and university administrators, have far too low standards for what a great course should be. A truly great course should immerse the students in fascinating and/or thorny situations in which they fully experience key elements of the subject matter, guiding students to actively use their mind and spirit to triumph over those situations, often inspiring them to exclaim, "Aha!"

I am aware that it is not easy to create nor teach such a course but that and nothing less should be the goal.

Key to that is to look for instructors outside academe. People who opt to get a Ph.D. are unlikely to be transformational instructors: Ph.D. students are people who have deliberately opted out of the real world for "a life of the mind." And if those Ph.D. students don't start graduate school focused on trivia, graduate school and the professoriate's reward structure makes most of them that way.

The best undergraduate instructors are likely to have these characteristics:

- Caring more about elevating than informing their students.

- Are *not* natural geniuses in the subject matter. The brilliant mathematician rarely can help typical students learn to reason well quantitatively in their daily life, to use cost-benefit/risk-reward analysis in decision-making. More likely to do so is an instructor who struggled to get an A in quantitative reasoning but now really "gets it" and reasons well quantitatively in her daily life.

- A bright but not brilliant student who has just a bachelor's degree. Too great a disparity between students' and instructor's ability and knowledge base reduces the likelihood of that instructor transforming the student.

- Is theatrical. It is difficult for many students to remain focused even on a five-minute mini-lecture. The ability to be a compelling storyteller is a real plus but lectures are very rarely transformative. So the instructor must have the restraint to use even the most fascinating lecturettes only as a spice, not as the main course.

- Should often use immersive simulation --for example, putting students in the role of the general in a Civil War battle, a surgeon deciding where and how to cut, an investor deciding where to invest his life's savings, a disaster relief manager deciding how to allocate resources.

Of course, such instructors are difficult to find. That's why I so believe *the* way to improve the quality of education worldwide is to find such people, have them develop those highly immersive courses, and distribute them online, the *dream-team-taught courses* I mentioned earlier and describe in detail in the next reinvention.

Require each college to post a report card on itself

Despite college being among our largest and most important purchases, the government provides us with less consumer information than we get before buying tires, which have a "report card" molded into each sidewall, or packaged food, which must list its contents from Vitamin A to zinc.

Especially with the spate of reports[127] demonstrating the frighteningly small-value added and employability that today's college graduates derive, each college should be required, on its website, to post a Report Card on itself. It need include just six items:

- The projected four- and five-year full cost of attendance, including cash financial aid, broken down by family income and assets.

- Freshman-to-senior average growth in critical thinking, writing, and quantitative reasoning, broken down by high school record.
- The results of the college's most recent student satisfaction survey.
- Four-, five-, and six-year graduation rates, broken down by high school record.
- The accreditation team's most recent report on the college.
- The percentage of graduates professionally employed, including average salary, disaggregated by high school record and by major.

To reduce cheating, the report cards would be externally audited.

Mandating that colleges post such a report card would, of course, help students select a college wisely or even decide that, given their academic record, motivation, and finances, a non-college option, for example, an apprenticeship program, would be wiser.

As important, making transparent the poor value-added most colleges provide would embarrass them into improving their quality of education. For example, they'd likely replace some of their many insignificant-research-focused professors with outstanding teachers. They'd reallocate some of their athletic and shrub budget to providing peer and adult mentors for students as well as to a career center that actually got students jobs.

To comment, click HERE[128].

26
DREAM-TEAM-TAUGHT COURSES

Education circles are atwitter about KhanAcademy.com lessons because they enable anyone to get clearly explained lessons, for example, in algebra. But they're boring. For the most part, they consist of a voice explaining the numbers and formulas shown on a blackboard. And they're isolated lessons, not a full course.

A far better approach is what I call, *Dream-Team-Taught Courses*. They would give every student, rich and poor, from Harlem to Beverly Hills, access to world-class courses.

Instead of high school students being taught by a random teacher, each student in the class, on a tablet or notebook computer, would receive, streamed from the Internet, lecturettes delivered by a dream-team of the nation's most transformational instructors, supplemented by first-rate visuals, immersive simulations, and assessments. Each concept would be taught at three paces: fast, medium, and slow.

The lecturettes would be subtitled and/or translated into other languages, especially Spanish.

A live teacher or paraprofessional would be in each classroom to help each student select the right pace, to answer questions, and provide supplementation.

Alternatively, the students could watch the videos at home and, in class, receive a full class period of support from the teacher. This is called the *flipped classroom*[129].

How would the dream team of teachers be recruited?

Invitations would be issued to state and national Teachers of the Year. Also, Internet-posted videos would be reviewed to identify teachers that seem to have "the magic." And queries to education leaders would be made requesting a referral to a teacher who meets these criteria:

- excellent at explaining concepts.

- able to teach those concepts differently but equally well to fast learners and slower learners.

- able to make kids like the subject, even kids who heretofore disliked it.

- his/her classes' scores on standardized tests consistently significantly exceed the expected score. Each applicant would have to provide evidence that her or his students' scores did so. Applicants would also submit a video of him or her teaching the relevant subject. Finalists would be asked to submit an outline for the portion of the course s/he would teach, and give permission for us to contact their students, parents, and administrators for references.

How would dream-team-taught courses work in practice?

Because some teachers would resist having someone other than themselves deliver the lecturettes, the live teachers could elect to themselves deliver some or even all of the lecturettes, and use the internet-based Dream-Team-Teacher's lecturettes and the supplementary material only as desired, for example, as homework.

As a concomitant benefit, teachers watching those Dream-Team-Taught lecturettes is a just-in-time form of professional development.

Note that the *Dream-Team Course* paradigm has been designed with teachers unions in mind. The unions are concerned about adding workload to teachers and about potential loss of teaching jobs. Dream-Team Courses make it easier for teachers to provide high-quality differentiated instruction, and are better implemented with a teacher rather than a paraprofessional in the room.

I am directing development of a mini-version of a Dream-Team-Taught Algebra 1 course. It will be piloted in a Napa County public school in fall, 2012.

To comment, click HERE[130]

27
CLOSING THE ACHIEVEMENT GAP

No domestic issue has drawn more attention or money than attempting to close the socioeconomic and racial achievement gap.

Now, despite a half century and countless innovations from Head Start to Stop Drop, from integration to self-segregated Afrocentric schools, from affirmative action college admission to disparate impact lawsuits on CEO selection, the achievement gap remains as wide as ever.

Even Head Start, which politicians for decades, trumpeted as our best hope, has recently been determined, in the definitive evaluation of 40 years of Head Start conducted by the U.S. Office of Education[131], to have no enduring positive effects.

So it would be hubristic of me to assert that I know how to close the achievement gap but we need to keep trying. So if I were to bet my money, these are the interventions I'd bet on:

1. Reduce teen pregnancy. It's well established that children of teenage parents are at greater risk of school and life failure. So junior and senior high schools, especially those with high teen pregnancy rates, should implement data-driven teen-pregnancy prevention programs[132]. The research does not support abstinence-only programs and so political pressures to restrict such programs to abstinence-only should be resisted.

Sex education should include what I call a *Choose Your Parent Well* component. You can't choose your parents but you certainly can be wise or less wise in choosing the parent of your children. **The decision of whom to be the father/mother of your children may be your life's most important.** Especially among at-risk teens, there's a tendency to fall in love with a person more on how "cool" than on how intelligent and psychologically healthy s/he is. But is that the person whose genes you'd like your child to have? Is that the person you want to parent your child?

To ensure that girls have the child with the father they want, when they're ready, birth control, including <u>long-term reversible implantables</u>[133] should be made available free, on demand, at all high schools.

Creators of programming aimed at teens (sitcoms, news, movies, video games, music videos, record labels) should be encouraged to create more content that would compellingly display the *Choose Your Parent Well* message as well as the non-romantic outcomes of teen pregnancy.

2. Provide parenting education early. To increase the chances that from Day One, parents have the tools to be good parents, full effort should be expended to ensure that high-quality parenting education is highly accessible, especially to pregnant teens in low-income locales.

The best parenting education involves interactive video of critical incidents in parenting--for example, what to do if your baby won't stop crying? What to do to ensure your child develops good language skills? Ethics? What if your child won't do homework? What if you think your child is taking drugs? Is sexually active?

True innovation in delivery systems is required. For example, high school websites and others heavily visited by at-risk teens, for example, mtv.com, should be encouraged to post the aforementioned parenting training course.

To ensure its availability to people without computers, the community center in low-income housing projects should have a computer installed that includes the parenting education program as well as other interactive-video programs, for example, on teen pregnancy prevention and on preventing and curing substance abuse. In hospitals, especially those serving at-risk communities, the TV in each new-mom's patient's room should have a TV offering the aforementioned parenting training.

To receive welfare benefits such as TANF funds, teen or perhaps all parents should be required to successfully complete the online or an in-person parenting education course, much as we require aspiring drivers to complete a driver's education course.

3. Improve teacher training. Absurdly, pre-K to grade-12 teachers are trained primarily by theory-oriented academics who have never taught in a pre-K to grade-12 classroom, let alone been master teachers there. That must change. The primary instructors of teachers in-training should be master K-12 teachers, including those who have produced excellent results in teaching low-achieving students.

Teachers of classes in low-achieving schools may well need to be masters at motivation, using a skill set beyond what is taught in most teacher education programs. So, for example, the increasingly required multicultural education course should include master-teacher-taught lessons on the art of classroom management, including strategies particularly likely to be effective in working with low-achieving, minimally motivated kids.

Training should not end upon the teacher's obtaining a license to teach. Teachers experiencing the frustrations common in working in low-achieving schools should be able to phone or email a hotline staffed by teachers who have successfully taught in those schools.

4. Flexibly group classes. If I were a slow learner and choosing between a class filled with other slow learners and a class with many hotshots, I'd certainly choose the former. Yet largely because minorities were overrepresented in the slow-learner classes, K-8 students are increasingly assigned to classes at random. That causes all students to suffer: It's nearly impossible for a teacher to meet the needs of a class with so wide-ranging needs. We must stop policies that are created merely to look good racially. Pedagogy must trump politics.

Classes shouldn't be rigidly tracked but we do need what I call *flex classes*. In them, at least for academic subjects, students are grouped by ability and achievement but in which students, especially those of color, are monitored closely to ensure they're not in a too low- (or too high-) level class.

5. Dispel the belief that working hard is **"acting white[134]."** Berkeley researcher John Ogbu is one of many to report that many black students believe that being studious is "acting white," and therefore is unacceptable. "Cool" blacks, both peers and adults, who are studious, must convince students and their parents that studying hard is equally important for students of all races.

6. Encourage an internal locus of control. Of course, what happens to us is not totally under our control. We are greatly affected by the family and community into which we are born. We are affected by the nature of the political and economic system under which we live. There is racism. There is reverse racism. There is luck.

Yet successful people believe they can control enough of their life to increase their chances of success. Academics call that *internal locus of control.* Alas, students from low-income families are more likely to believe that external factors such as luck, God, and their race are key to determining their success.

Moving poor people's locus of control inward is no easy task. Many political leaders, educators, and TV pundits gain popularity by telling their audiences that their failings are largely beyond their control: the capitalist system, the legacy of slavery, institutional racism, white privilege, etc. Clerics urge, "God will provide!"

While those may be partially responsible, our mind molders--parents, schools, colleges, church, and media--would be wise to encourage all of us to base our self-esteem, our sense of self-efficacy, on what we ourselves do. The accomplishments of famous people or people of our race should *not* be a particular source of pride. Our own efforts, accomplishments, ethics, and kindness should be the primary bases for assessing our self-worth.

7. Chronically disruptive students should be placed in special classes. If a student, despite the teacher's best efforts with help from the principal, continues to disrupt classmates' opportunity to learn, that child should be moved to a special class taught by someone with special skills in working with such kids. Even if that child does no better in that special class, s/he won't be depriving the other 29 students of their right to an education.

8. Begin career exploration in middle school. Finding an exciting yet realistic career can motivate many students. And it reduces the problem of many high school and college graduates having no idea of what career they want to pursue.

8a. Internships starting in middle school? I'd like to see a pilot program in which internships and apprenticeships begin being offered in middle school.

9. Give students a choice: college-prep or direct-to-career curriculum. This was recommended in an earlier section of this book but it likely is of particular value in closing the achievement gap, so I revisit that here.

Increasingly, in the name of high standards, high schoolers, even those who read on a 6th-grade level and who have far more ability in working with their hands, are being forced to take a college-prep curriculum.

Imagine that you, like millions of parents, have a child entering high school who's reading on just a 6th-grade level. Would you want him forced to take a curriculum that required him to master trigonometry, the details of the Louisiana Purchase, and write essays on Wuthering Heights? He'll almost certainly do terribly. Not surprisingly, mandating a one-size-fits-all curriculum causes many to drop out of high school[135].

Worse, the child won't have had an opportunity to build the basic survival skills--reading, writing, critical thinking and math--he'll desperately need and doesn't yet have. He could better learn those in a direct-to-career path, for example a health-care or entrepreneurship academy within the high school. But as with ability-grouped classes, direct-to-career high school paths have largely been eliminated. Indeed one of President Obama's top domestic priorities is "Some college for all."

Today, many colleges are open-admission even to the grossly underprepared. Alas, if a student is one of the 200,000 per year entering so-called 4-year colleges from the bottom 40% of their high school class, their chances of graduating are only 24%, even if given 8 1/2 years! And if they do defy the odds and graduate, it will likely be with a low grade-point average in an major such as sociology, art, or physical education from a minimally selective college. That will impress few employers at a time when the U.S. has the highest percentage of college graduates in its history at the same time as employers are eliminating as many professional-level positions as possible, through automation, offshoring, or converting jobs to part-time and temp positions. Such graduates are likely to join the 53 percent of people[136] under 25 with a bachelor's degree unable to find better employment than they could have found with just a high school diploma.

Meanwhile they have incurred large student debt, boredom, and ongoing assault to self-esteem from being forced to study academic material for which they were unprepared and uninterested.

If my child had struggled unsuccessfully through middle school, I'd rather see him improve his reading, writing, thinking, and mathematical reasoning in high school courses that would prepare him to be, for example, an entrepreneur, robotics tech, helicopter pilot, or chef.

A high-quality, not dumping-ground, direct-to-career option should be instituted in high schools, especially those schools serving many students whose academic achievement is below grade-level.

It's ironic that the leaders who most claim to celebrate diversity are the most likely to insist on no diversity in the high school curriculum: they want *everyone* to take a college-preparatory curriculum to "keep students' options open." Ironically, one-size-fits-all education eliminates excellent options.

10. Require a course in life skills. Before requiring at-risk kids, indeed all kids, to learn to plot parabolas, the halide elements, and the use of the doppelganger, students should be required to pass a course in life skills: for example, budgeting, interpersonal communication, and the aforementioned sex education and parenting education. To not do so is to be guilty of the very elitism that many educators and politicians decry.

11. Institute a debate program in all high schools, including those with low achievement scores. Some evidence[137] and a lot of common sense suggests that a debate program could yield significant benefit.

12. Require colleges to provide full disclosure to prospective students. In their attempt to woo students, especially students of color, colleges and high school counselors, as in the Tuskegee Experiments, often hide the information students need to use to decide whether to enroll:

- The projected four- and five-year full cost of attendance, including cash financial aid, broken down by family income and assets.

- Freshman-to-senior average growth in critical thinking, writing, and quantitative reasoning, broken down by high school record.

- The results of the college's most recent student satisfaction survey

- Four-, five-, and six-year graduation rates, broken down by high school record.

- The accreditation team's most recent report on the college.

- The percentage of graduates professionally employed, including average salary, disaggregated by high school record and by major.

13. *Head Start Genes.* Our intelligence and impulse control are, like nearly all characteristics in the animal and plant kingdom, likely affected by both our genes and our environment. Yet the government and biotech companies have--for fear of political repercussions--been reluctant to fund research that would identify which gene clusters are responsible for those characteristics. Government should encourage such research so prospective parents could have ***the option*** of having their eggs and sperm tested to ensure their baby will be born with genes for good intelligence and impulse control so s/he doesn't start out life with a strike or two against them. We already do this on a crude basis: In in-vitro fertilization, the physician chooses only eggs and sperm that appear normal and robust. If *all* of a prospective mother's and father's genes are for low intelligence or impulse control, the parents should have the option of having the defective genes in their egg and sperm replaced with normal ones, what I call *Head Start genes*.

To ensure that the poor has access to this procedure, it would, like other medical procedures, be covered under MediCal and other health programs for the poor. In addition, as with, for example, AIDS education, special outreach would be made in low-income communities to ensure that its residents are aware of the *Head Start genes* option.

Because low-income people are, on average, at the low end of the achievement gap, they would likely benefit far more from *Head Start genes* than would the pool of high achievers.

14. Try pilot studies. In addition to implementing the previous ideas, there's need to pilot test new ideas. Examples:

- For those unable to hold a private-sector job, government should create jobs. A job may be, in addition to a source of income, the most potent teacher, healer, and crime and drug abuse preventer.

- Pair high school kids with retired small business owners. Have them start a simple business.

- Pair at-risk kids with nursing home residents or hard-to-adopt animal-shelter dogs and cats that otherwise would be euthanized. I've seen hard-bitten teens grow loving when involved with a non-threatening person or animal.

- Have kids plant vegetable and fruit gardens, cook and eat what they've grown and sell the rest. They'd learn science, cooking, nutrition, and how to run a business. In addition, they might join me in awe of the miracle of growth.

- Create peer-mentor pairs: for example, at-risk sixth graders with at-risk first graders. Teaching it is a good way to learn it.

- Provide free genetic counseling to at-risk prospective parents. That may help them make more fully informed and thus wiser choices.

My hope is that this more thorough exploration of how to address the achievement gap might encourage a more full-dimensioned discussion than the nation has heretofore had. I believe that without such a discussion, we'll still be wringing our hands about the achievement gap a century from now.

To comment, click HERE[138].

28
FINANCIAL AID, REINVENTED

MAKE COLLEGES EARN IT

Studies have made clear colleges' unconscionably bad value-added[139]: growth in student learning, personal development, and of course, employability.

For example, rigorous research have revealed that college students learn shockingly little. Just one of many such studies, in _Academically Adrift[140]_, it was reported that **36% of graduating seniors nationwide grew not at all in problem solving, critical thinking, and analytical reasoning since entering college as freshmen!**

And our sending the highest percentage of students to college in history (now 70%) has created an oversupply of college graduates. That helps explains why, according to a Pew fiscal analysis, **35 percent of the unemployed with college or graduate degrees have been unemployed for more than a year, the same rate as unemployed high school dropouts!**

The government would never allow a drug to be sold, let alone subsidize it, without the drug's manufacturer demonstrating its efficacy. Yet colleges receive enormous sums of taxpayer dollars, and the government keeps increasing financial aid, which allows colleges to raise tuitions higher and put yet more money in their coffers. So even in these tight times, colleges are getting rewarded with ever more of our tax dollars for their terrible performance

A way of getting colleges to (finally) change

It's time for a change. **Before receiving taxpayer-paid financial aid, each college should be required to demonstrate freshman-to-senior growth in learning and employability that even minimally justifies the four to eight years, enormous cost, and risk of not graduating**. Nationwide, fewer than 40% of first-time freshmen graduate within four years. Fewer than two-thirds graduate even if given six years!

Putting a little flesh on that skeleton, I believe that, to receive taxpayer-funded financial-aid dollars, all colleges be required to demonstrate:

91

1) At least modest average-student growth in critical thinking, analytic reasoning, and problem solving as measured by a standardized exam selected by a national blue-ribbon panel of psychometricians, higher educators, and employers. Well-validated such instruments exist, for example, the Collegiate Learning Assessment[141].

2) At least modestly improved employability of the institution's graduates. The Bureau of Labor Statistics has long categorized jobs in terms of how much education is typically required. Colleges should demonstrate they can abet employability. For example:

<3.0/50 percentile on SAT: 25% of graduates are employed in a position requiring more than a high school diploma within one year of graduation, or are in graduate school

3.25/65 percentile SAT: 40% of graduates are employed requiring more than a high school diploma within one year of graduation, or are in graduate school

3.50/80 percentile SAT: 55% of graduates are employed requiring more than a high school diploma within one year of graduation or are in graduate school

3.75/90 percentile SAT: 70% of graduates are employed in a position requiring more than a high school diploma within one year of graduation, or are in graduate school.

Most experts contend that a better-educated citizenry is key to a better America. To date, we have given higher education a free pass and mammoth access to our tax dollars while requiring less accountability than we do for a tire. That must screech to a halt.

To comment, click HERE[142].

29
THE COLLEGE CAMPUS SHOULD GO EXTINCT

I don't understand why the college campus, with its monumental costs and inconvenient access, continues to exist.

Entities should be created to aggregate

course credits and award degrees, with students able to take courses anywhere (in-person in individual hotel rooms, apartments, and, where necessary, classrooms and labs) and offered by professional associations, private education companies, and yes, traditional colleges and universities.

I understand that traditionally, high school graduates view the campus experience as a halfway house between living with their parents and independent adulthood, but the price has become absurd: More than $200,000 sticker price[143] for four years at brand-name private colleges--and *most* students take longer than four years. Yet students, ever afraid to not do what their friends do, go--after all, their parents are paying. And parents, nostalgic for their own college years, and not wanting to even be perceived as short-changing their child, suck it up, sacrifice their financial security and more, and pay the inconceivably large amount, or bury their head in the sand by taking on massive amount of student loan, practically the only loan--thanks to the higher education lobbying machine-- that is almost impossible to discharge in bankruptcy.

It is wrong that student fees subsidize universities' research, the vast majority of which is apriori known to be a terribly cost-ineffective use of student and taxpayer money. In addition, it's forced charity--much of the sticker price is redistributed to the poor, and to a lesser extent to athletes, "underrepresented" minorities, etc. It's also wrong that students and taxpayers be forced to pay for swimming pools, golf courses, etc. HERE is quite an example.

To comment, click HERE[144].

30
COLLEGES' GENERAL EDUCATION, REINVENTED

In theory, general education courses should be key to creating outstanding citizens and professionals, imbuing students with better critical thinking, leadership, and connoisseurship skills, a valuing of high ideals and the skills to bring them about.

Alas, most students think of general education as the irrelevant courses they have to "get out of the way" so they can get on with their major and electives, and get their diploma.

Here, I propose a reinvention of general education, not just in subject matter but in delivery.

GeneralEd.org would be a highly interactive general education program filled with content that the typical undergraduate would be eager to learn, taught on video by world-class instructors and available to colleges across the world to use with its students.

The courses' exams would tap crucial understandings and skills such as critical thinking yet would be multiple-choice so the entire program can be completed without the college or university providing any faculty. GeneralEd.org would be self-contained, turnkey.

Central to each GeneralEd.org course would be these features:

- The core screening criterion for course content: *Is that content central to the life well-led and unlikely to be adequately acquired outside of college?* Each course's primary focus would be to maximize the probability that the students will incorporate each course's core skills and knowledge into the way they function day-in- and day out, professionally and personally.
- Each course's instructor(s) would be on video, enabling every student, even if millions, from all across the globe, to receive a world-class instructor.
- The instructors, *drawn from within and outside academia,* would be selected on demonstrated ability to enable students to fully understand and use complicated but important concepts, motivate students to love learning, and, most important, be transformational: help students grow in important ways beyond learning the course material. I would reach out to selected state and national teachers and professors of the year but not be restricted to them.
- Courses would make generous use of true interactivity (role play, debate, simulation, reflecting on rhetorical questions) plus lecturettes with options to click on links to explanatory text, video, etc. Each instructor would develop the course in collaboration with an expert in creating courses on Moodle[145] or other top online course platform.
- There would be student-to-student online interaction: discussions about the lecturettes, group immersive projects, forums to address problems, etc.
- Iris or fingerprint recognition technology, questions embedded in course to verify participation, and open-book exams would reduce cheating to levels below that in traditional instruction.

GeneralEd.org, would not only be a boon to students but would solve critical problems faced by many institutions of higher education.

- Many institutions wish they could admit more freshmen but there's no room. GeneralEd.org would allow colleges to admit as many students as it wished *and* to provide a high-quality program. That will help address the additional enrollment pressures that will accrue, for example, because President Obama is calling for nearly everyone to have some college education. The cost to a college of GeneralEd.org would be low enough that at most institutions, regular student tuition would cover its cost.
- Many faculty don't enjoy teaching general education courses because the content is basic and/or because many students are insufficiently prepared or motivated to succeed in those courses. GeneralEd.org would free faculty to teach the more advanced courses they prefer and/or to devote more time to their research and service.

More than 70 semester credits worth of courses are listed below. Each institution could decide how much choice to allow students in selecting the courses that would meet that institution's general education requirement.

The Courses

THE LIFE WELL-LED (3 semester credits): Philosophies of living.

CHOOSING A CAREER (3 credits)

PRODUCTIVITY (3 credits) Study/learning skills, time management, stress management gaining motivation.

CRITICAL THINKING (3 credits)
Note: I provide more detail for this course for illustrative purposes.)
Structure: Students watch 50 ever more complicated arguments in text, speeches and debates (drawn heavily from YouTube) and make moment-to-moment judgments of the quality of argumentation and then compare them against the instructor's moment-by-moment judgments. 30-second to five-minute lecturettes will be inserted between video clips to highlight a critical thinking principle embedded in one of the videos. Example: how to avoid getting seduced by the presenter's style rather than the substance.

Categories from which clips will be drawn:
- Advertising

- Workplace: e.g., sexism, whether to market a new product, an approach to fundraising, salary negotiation.
- Debates on core societal problems: world poverty, global terrorism, improving the U.S. educational system, the federal deficit, our election system, improving the U.S. economy in an era of China's and India's ascendance, societal lack of ethics, diversity issues.
- Analyzing policy arguments: e.g., climate change, the racial achievement/income gap
- Analyzing political arguments: e.g., liberal, conservative, libertarian, socialist.

Examinations: Students will take exams assessing their critical thinking skills. Sample item: Here are four one-paragraph arguments. Put them in order, from strongest to weakest.

PROFESSIONAL COMMUNICATION (3 credits) (For Module I, I provide a sample of what a lesson might look like)

Module I: Keys to effective professional communication (This is the section on general communication skills. The conflict-prevention and conflict resolution sections are later.)

A. Show video of an effective communication between an employee and boss. Instead, you may wish to role-play both sides of the communication.
B. Explain that a key to those people's effectiveness were the strength and clarity of the reasoning. Then teach students a technique that would help them present more clearly and concisely: for example, you might have them pretend they have 60 seconds to explain something of life-or-death importance to a sixth grader. Have them practice the technique with their webcam. Have each student rate himself and video themselves again as much as s/he wants to--at least twice in order to get credit for completing that submodule.
C. Explain that the other key to communication effectiveness is style. Then teach them a technique or two that would quickly improve their style. For example, "Pretend you're not yourself but an actor you've seen on TV or in a movie who has just the right dynamism, tone quality, presence, etc. Imitate that person."

Use the same model (steps A, B, and C), but this time starting with a video of (or you role playing both sides of) an effective communication between two peers. At your discretion, you might want to repeat this process with other examples: perhaps employee and customer, or employee and vendor.

Students then must pass a five-to-ten-item exam you'd create before going on to the next module. While, for logistical reasons, it must be multiple-choice, it is critical that those items go well beyond testing facts. For example, a test item on this module's exam might consist of four five-second videos of you making a point. The student must rank-order them in order of effectiveness.

Module II: Conflict prevention
Module III: Conflict resolution
Module IV: Managing and leading people
Module V: Running a meeting
Module VI: Negotiation
Module VII: Writing a report
Module VIII: Writing an email
Module IX: Public speaking.

READING COMPREHENSION (bachelor's level) (3 credits)
Realistic fiction
Fantasy fiction
Narrative non-fiction (e.g., biographies, current events)
How-to non-fiction
Technical material (including owner's manuals and help screens)

WRITING (Bachelor's level) (3 credits)
The persuasive essay
Expository writing
Email
Writing for new media: blogs, Twitter, Facebook
The art of letter writing

QUANTITATIVE REASONING (3 credits)
(Incorporating risk-reward/probabilistic thinking in daily life.)

INTERPERSONAL COMMUNICATION (3 credits)
Communicating with friends.
Communicating with a romantic partner
Communicating with your family
Cross-cultural communication

ENTREPRENEURSHIP (3 credits)
The art and science of identifying unmet needs that could become successful businesses
How to start a lemonade stand
How to turn a lemonade stand into Joy Juice, Inc. (NASDAQ: joyj)

Social entrepreneurship

ETHICS (3 credits:)
Selfish and altruistic reasons why ethical behavior is core.
10 common, tempting ethical decisions
10 common, difficult ethical dilemmas

DIGITAL LITERACY (3 credits)
Email, texting
Using Windows, Mac, iPhone, and Android operating systems
Word processing
Spreadsheet
Database
File management
Troubleshooting
Digital audio (e.g., mp3)
Digital video (still cameras, videocams)

FINANCIAL LITERACY (3 credits)
Practical micro and macro economics
Developing a philosophy of spending versus saving
Savings: banks, bonds, stocks, mutual funds, etfs, real estate, tangible assets.
Deciding when you should borrow and how.
Your housing: Rent? Buy? How?
Your transportation: Car? Bicycle? Mass Transit? How to buy?
Your education: Another degree? How to choose?
Your food: Shopping wisely
Your clothing: Shopping wisely.
Time-effectively obtaining a good deal on smaller purchases
Wise charitable giving
Protecting yourself against scams

CRITICAL DECISIONS IN HISTORY (3 credits)
Students are the decisionmaker in simulations of, for example, whether the
U.S. should have invaded Iraq, entered World War II, responded to the
Cuban missile crisis, etc. Students debate other students.

LITERATURE APPRECIATION (3 credits)

ART APPRECIATION (3 credits)

MUSIC APPRECIATION (3 credits)

THEATRE APPRECIATION (2 credits)

FILM APPRECIATION (3 credits)
(including YouTube video)

VIDEOGAME APPRECIATION (2 credits)

SCIENCE FOR NON SCIENTISTS (3 credits)
Thinking scientifically in daily life. (College-level application of the scientific method, risk-reward analysis, etc.)

Students are the decisionmaker in simulations of key situations: what role if any should nuclear energy play
What should the U.S. do about climate change?
Is it worth funding proposal X for searching for a cure for sudden heart attack?
Should research that would use gene therapy to increase intelligence be illegal? Government funded?

CITIZENSHIP (3 credits)
What is the good citizen?
Comparing the major political philosophies: liberal, conservative, socialist, libertarian.
Economics for citizens: microeconomics, macroeconomics.
How government works.
Finding a compatible service opportunity

HEALTH (2 credits)
Diet, and finding the lifetime discipline
Exercise, and finding the lifetime discipline
Addictive drugs: alcohol, drugs, cigarettes
Minimizing and addressing anxiety, depression.
Visiting your physician: preparing, making the most of the appointment.

DOMESTIC ISSUES (2 credits)
Food preparation
Parenting
Aesthetics
Wise consumer purchasing

PUBLIC SPEAKING (3 credits)

LANDING A JOB (2 credits)

RECREATING WISELY (1 credit)

To comment, click <u>HERE</u>[146].

31
THE MEDIA REINVENTED

The media may be our most powerful societal influencer: It affects whom we elect, the laws that get passed, what we buy, nearly everything.

And today's media has tools to do an ever better job. For example, a journalist can crowd-source interviews with just a Twitter question. With their cell phones, citizens can instantly transmit video of news events to media outlets worldwide.

Journalists have worsened

But today's media has become less helpful to the public because it has often abandoned its near-sacred responsibility to provide a full range of benevolently derived perspectives on the issues of the day. Instead, reporting tends to reflect their apriori biases, which, per the below, which overwhelmingly are in a liberal direction

The core cause: journalism schools' change in philosophy. In previous generations, journalism schools taught its students to make all efforts to be fair and balanced. Now, the message is more often, "You have the opportunity to change the world." (that usually means increased redistribution.)

Alas, most journalists and their editors have spent little time in the real world. Their world view too heavily reflects what they learned in college, from their fellow journalists, and from their friends. Those influences tend to be overwhelmingly liberal: Academia is left-leaning, the people who enter journalism do so in part to change their world in that leftward direction, and they choose friends with similar views.

A *The Hill* poll[147] of 1,000 likely voters found that 68% consider the news media biased, with more than twice as many respondents believing the bias is leftward. Worse, 57% believe the news media is somewhat or very unethical while only 39 percent see them as somewhat or very ethical. In a Gallup poll,[148] only 26% rated journalists' ethics high or very high. 27% rated them as low or very low.

And it's not that the public is inaccurate in perceiving the media to be biased. UCLA, no conservative bastion, reports[149] that "almost all major media outlets tilt to the left."

Fox News, the only major conservative outlet, is so ridiculed by the other media that it now gets only a small mindshare of the public, especially among the intelligentsia, those most likely to vote and to influence policy.

Yes, much wisdom comes from left of center, but not all, but you wouldn't know that from the media. Not only do article topics and approaches to those topics tend to be left-biased, freelance articles and op-eds with right-of-center perspectives are generally rejected, censored, as are right-of-center books and movies submitted for review.

The media exerts its liberal bias in ways other than censorship, for example, a double-standard. In my years of reading reviews, it seems clear to me that right-of-center or libertarian contentions are scrutinized for methodological rigor far more microscopically than are liberal contentions.

Here are more examples of the double standard:

Recall, for instance, how the media destroyed Newt Gingrich by relentlessly reminding us of an old affair and by making exaggerated claims of his pomposity while giving Obama a free pass on his hubristic certitude that massive debt increases and redistributive "justice" is wise.

When George Bush decided "No New Taxes" was unwise, the media excoriated him as a flip-flopper. Yet when Obama changed from being against gay marriage to for it, the media extolled him.

The media also gives Obama free passes on Big Lies. For example, he forced taxpayers to spend $60 billion to bail out GM, a company that makes inferior cars, and he now claims that has paid off. In fact, GM's stock price has plummeted from 34 before the bailout to 20 as of this writing. The breakeven point is 53[150]. The taxpayer has lost $16 billion.

A broader example: Obama claims he's bringing the economy back. Not according to this[151] chart. Obama bragged relentlessly about millions of shovel-ready jobs that weren't, yet the media has pretty much ignored that inconvenient fiction. Articles calling Obama to account are relegated to conservative websites. For example, the National Review reported[152] that the taxpayer will have spent at least $185,000 for *each* job created by Obama's "stimulus" spending.

The media gave Obama a free pass for saying the U.S. has 57 states while destroying Dan Quayle for misspelling "potato." The media endlessly trumpets Rush Limbaugh's drug problem, but when Edward Kennedy admitted to being an alcoholic and womanizer, it was downplayed, now brushed aside as ancient history.

The media exerts its bias in countless other ways, including the subtle. For example, when George Bush was president, the media so often called him "Bush," whereas it mainly calls Obama "The President." The media has adopted the Left's focus-group-tested self-descriptor "progressive" rather than "liberal." After all, "liberal" implies a tendency to overspend whereas "progressive" has a positive connotation. Who could be against progress? Regressives?

Journalism that opens minds
It's time for a new core principle of journalism: That journalists indeed have a near-sacred responsibility to present a wide range of intelligent, benevolently derived ideas, to be the grist for full-dimensioned citizen conversations about the issues of our time.

For example, **there are solid arguments for and against wealth redistribution, for and against Keynesianism, for and against undertaking massive efforts to cool the planet, for and against America's continuing as the world's policeman. Consumers of the media should not have to make far greater effort to find best-made cases for right-of-center and libertarian ideas than for left-of-center ones.**

In my view, few things could improve America more than a media that opens rather than closes minds.

To comment, click HERE[153].

REINVENTIONS OF RELATIONSHIPS

32

REINVENTING HOW WE CHOOSE STUDENTS, EMPLOYEES, POLITICIANS, AND ROMANTIC PARTNERS

We're always selecting people, for example:

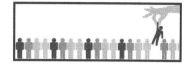

- whom to admit to a selective school or college

- whom to hire or promote

- whom to vote for

- whom to date

Wise selection is critical to the nation. For example, consider the importance of whom we choose to admit to prestigious education institutions, from top preschools to top post-doc programs. Those are door-openers to leadership and to top professional positions. In employment, choose people who are less skilled, hard-working, ethical, unintelligent and/or high-maintenance, and society suffers. Choosing our spouse and the parent of our children affects our lives and our next generation.

It's important to choose people wisely even in seemingly mundane situations. For example, hiring the right middle manager at a widget company improves his/her supervisees' quality of life and helps ensure that a quality widget is produced and can be sold affordably. That benefits all the customers. Multiply that across a nation and you can see how important it is that we select people wisely.

Alas, we too often select poorly. We rely heavily on invalid criteria:

- Looks.

- Professional licensure exams are the gatekeeper for our professionals from our haircutters and Realtors to our psychologists, lawyers and doctors. Alas, those exams, developed heavily by out-of-touch ivory-tower professors, too often test arcana that have little to do with competence on the job.

- Resumes often are inflated and/or represent the thinking and writing ability of a hired-gun resume writer rather than the candidate's. And even if accurate, what a resume highlights--academic qualifications and length of job experience--are poor predictors of workplace success.

- References are often puffery: Candidates offer only references who will say positive things, even if they have to ask their sweetie to pretend s/he was his boss.

- Often, selection is based heavily on an interview and its analogue in politics, the speech. Why? Because we tend to trust what we personally experience more than, for example, a test score. Unfortunately, interviews and speechmaking are coachable and so, often we select the most coached applicant rather than one who'd be best on the job. Indeed, research[154] indicates that interviews too often lead to bad decisions.

Better approaches to employee selection and professional licensure

Of course, tests have their limitations. We all know people who scored high on the SAT, GRE, intelligence tests, etc., whom you wouldn't hire as a dog catcher. But predictive validity studies, for example, this one on how well tests of cognitive ability predict job performance[155], and this one[156] on how well the SAT predicts college grades, suggest that those tests (which correlate highly with each other) should be *one* criterion in selecting students or professional-level employees. Those tests are proxies for the ability to learn quickly, solve problems, and think abstractly, all of which are critical in all but low-level work. And racism and sexism are less likely on a test than in subjective judgment.

Those tests of cognitive ability must be distinguished from tests of personality, for example, the Myers Briggs, the Enneagram, etc., which have poor validity.

Beyond cognitive ability, how does one wisely assess other critical attributes of candidates: skill at the tasks s/he'll be doing, drive, emotional intelligence, flexibility, reliability, being emotionally low-maintenance?

Employee selection tests, including licensure exams, should consist largely of simulations of common situations the professional would face on the job. That would not only yield better-selected professionals, it would pressure the training institutions to replace their often professor-developed, trivia-centric curriculum with material more likely to develop good practitioners.

Similarly, selection interviews should minimize coachable questions such as, "Tell me about yourself?" "What are your greatest weaknesses," and "Tell me about a problem you faced?" Instead, interviews should focus on putting the candidate in simulations of situations s/he'll commonly face on the job. For example, graduate school applicants might be asked to participate in a classroom discussion, manager applicants to run a brief simulated meeting with their supervisees, scientists to design an experiment. Political candidates, in addition to the standard televised debate, should be asked to run a meeting with mock legislators.

References are notoriously unreliable. You're more likely to obtain valid references by using this approach: Before hiring someone, leave voice mail for ten past bosses and coworkers including those not listed as a reference, saying, "I'm hiring for a very important position. Jane Jones has applied. If you think she's wonderful, call me. If not, no need to." Unless you get at least six callbacks, you probably shouldn't hire Jane.

Hire for a trial period. Select the person for a trial day or week so you can both assess if you're right for each other. If the person balks, agree that if that first weeks goes satisfactorily, the position automatically is converted to a "permanent" one.

A word about using race or gender as a selection criterion. In the case of two equal candidates, in some cases, it can make sense to let diversity be the tie breaker but, too often, the price paid for a "diversity pick" is greater than the benefit derived: The selected candidate is known, upfront to be less likely than another candidate to make the most valuable contribution. Relegating merit to the back seat is, of course, unfair to more meritorious applicants and engenders resentment from them and from the public. Perhaps more important, it hurts society because it brings about worse goods and services for all of us: worse doctors, more poorly constructed bridges, inferior financial advisors, less safe airline pilots, less reliable products, worse customer service, etc.

Picking a romantic partner

Of course, more of the ineffable is involved in choosing a romantic partner, but couples would be happier if they at least considered how a potential long-term partner scores on this *Partner Report Card:*

- Compatibility in bed. Mismatched sex drive is among the most difficult-to-fix relationship problems.
- Compatibility out of bed. How much do you enjoy spending time with this person in non-sexual situations?
- Mutual respect. Do you view your partner as ethical, kind, intelligent enough, etc?
- Absence of a fatal flaw: alcoholism/drug addiction, violent temper, etc.
- Feeling: Even after the initial glow of infatuation has ebbed, you feel good being around this person.

Not only would using such a Partner Report Card help create happier couples, I predict it would create a better nation. I'd imagine that people who are content in their romantic relationship tend to be better on their jobs, with their friends, and as citizens.

To comment, click HERE[157].

33
PARENTING REINVENTED

Judith Rich Harris, author of The Nurture Assumption summarizes the research[158] that now suggests that parenting may less influence a child than genetics and peers.
Nevertheless, parenting, of course, is important to the child and to America's future.

And parenting isn't easy. Even most well-educated parents find parenting difficult. Indeed, many children of educated parents drive their parents crazy and/or grow up to be disappointments to their parents. That is even more prevalent among the poor.

If we require teens to take a course before they can drive, shouldn't we require a course before people become parents? For example, why not have a parenting education course replace one semester of physical education?

But even if that's not required, if all pre-parents, during their prenatal visits to the doctor, were taught just some rules of good parenting, it could improve the quality of parenting and reduce parental stress.

Of course, there are the obvious parenting musts, for example, talking to and reading to your young child, and being a careful diagnostician of why your baby is crying and responding appropriately. But there's a principle that is less obvious yet helpful to effective parenting: the use of guilt.

Lest that sound cruel or the narrow thinking of the stereotypical Jewish parent or Catholic cleric, let me explain. A core goal of parenting is to get the child to do the "right thing," not for of fear of reprisal but because, intrinsically, the child wants to do it. Yelling at or punishing a misbehaving child doesn't make the child intrinsically want to do the task. On the contrary, while it may temporarily quell the bad behavior, it engenders resentment so, in the future, the child is more likely to do something else bad to show he has the power. If, instead, when, for example, a child refuses to do his homework, the parent says, "Of course, that's up to you. You have to decide whether you want to be a responsible person, doing his job, which is homework, or you want to be a lazy person. You have to decide whether you want to be the person who learns things and gets smarter from doing homework, or who doesn't." Then, if the child doesn't slink off to do the homework, the parent simply sighs and walks away. No confrontation, no escalating power plays, less stress, and a child more likely to internalize positive values.

Yes, for some children, that is insufficient. Some kids do need tangible rewards and withdrawal of privileges. After all, how many of us would go to work if we didn't get a paycheck?

A word about corporal punishment: bad. Not only is it the most potent way to trigger the aforementioned escalating power struggle, it powerfully conveys that violence is an appropriate response. So when a classmate, or later, a romantic partner, does something your child doesn't like, s/he'll consider violence appropriate.

America is already too filled with people doing good only because of rewards and punishment rather than because it's the right thing to do. The U.S. is also riddled with violence. Whatever impact genes may have, it's hard not to believe that parenting isn't a powerful preventive.

34
FAMILY IS OVERRATED

Politicians, clerics, and just plain folks extol family as our most important institution. Yet as individuals, and as a nation, I believe we'd be wise to ask ourselves if, in our particular family, we'd be wise to reallocate our human and fiscal resources elsewhere.

So many people suffer inordinately from family. Of course, there are the obvious examples:

- child abuse
- domestic violence
- incest
- psychological abuse

More often, there's less dramatic but still painful family-induced misery:

- Other than pleasantries, your adult child refuses to speak with you.
- Your spouse has fallen out of love with you, yet fear, inertia, and shared history preclude a dissolution. So you trudge along.
- Your parent is still trying to control or demean you even though you're already an adult.
- Your nine-year-old regularly screams, "I hate you, mommy!"
- Your adult child is back on your sofa still trying to "find himself" (with the assistance of drugs or alcohol.)
- You're not capable enough to compete with a sibling or parent, which dispirits you.
- You make major efforts to care for your aging parent. Privately, you resent how much time, energy, and money it takes.
- Your spouse doesn't earn enough income or do enough around the house.
- You suffer the effects of an impaired, alcoholic, drug-abusing, gambling, or just plain lazy, parasitic family member.

Millions of people spend years and fortunes on therapists trying to undo the ills that family perpetrated on them.

All this shouldn't be surprising. After all, unlike with friends, we are placed in our family of origin at random, with no say in the matter. We do choose our spouse but hormones seem to preclude our doing a very good job of it-- witness America's 50% divorce rate[159].

While it's unseemly to discuss, money is part of the equation as we evaluate whether family is overrated. It costs a fortune to support kids, let alone a stay-at-home spouse. To pay for it, many people choose lucrative careers that are far less enjoyable than those they'd otherwise choose. Do you think that, if it weren't for the need to support a family, as many people would choose to sell insurance, be pest control workers, sewer repairers, or bond traders? Wouldn't many of them choose a career, for example, in the creative arts, in a nonprofit, or as a computer game maker?

Of course, I can envision some readers thinking:

"What? Are you advocating a society without children?" Encouraging my readers to think more carefully before having children is hardly going to lead to a world without children. I am merely asking people to be more circumspect, not reflexively fulfilling society's expectation. Besides, environmentalists argue that overpopulation is the greatest threat to the environment[160]. A few less children wouldn't hurt the world and its seven billion people.

"Life is even more difficult to live without the support of family." I'm not saying that people don't need support. I'm arguing against the automatic assumption that you have greater obligation to support family members than others. For example, when your ne'er-do-well sibling asks you for money because he or she is unemployed, rather than succumb to the reflexive guilt that society imposes because "he's family," you'd be wise to view the issue in fuller dimension: in terms of the net effects on you, him, your family, and, yes, society. For example, does giving Sam the Slug the money yield a greater net good than, for example, investing in a startup developing a drug to prevent sudden heart attack, the leading killer?

My main message is to resist automatically succumbing to convention, and instead, to make your choices consciously, based on what will ultimately yield the greatest good *en toto:* for you, your family, and society.

To comment, click HERE[161].

35
AN ALTERNATIVE TO COUPLES COUNSELING

Your relationship is doing poorly. Before heading to couples counseling, you might try what I call *The Couple's Council.*

It has helped a number of my clients, and frankly, my own marriage. One of my clients called it "The Ten-Minute Miracle."

Step 1: Perhaps over dinner, propose one specific thing you'll do during the next 24 hours to improve the relationship; for example, you're tired of your partner's procrastination, nagging, or being a pig. Your partner agrees that would at least modestly improve your relationship, or s/he asks you to propose something else. You keep proposing changes in your behavior until s/he okays one.

Step 2: You reverse roles. In other words, this step is completed when you agree that something your partner proposes to do would at least modestly improve your relationship.

Step 3: During the next 24 hours, when each of you sees your partner doing the desired behavior, for example, getting something done when s/he'd otherwise likely procrastinate, the person gets a thumbs-up. Each screw-up gets a thumbs-down but no lecture, no recriminations.

Step 4: 24 hours later, each of you rates him/herself on how well s/he did in improving on the agreed-on behavior. Then, you decide whether, in the next 24 hours, you want to work just on the same behavior or add another one.

Repeat the process until enough improvements have been made, or you decide you should see that couples counselor after all.

To comment, click HERE[162].

36
PSYCHOTHERAPY REINVENTED

Psychotherapy is expensive, time-consuming, and too often doesn't work well enough. It needs to be reinvented or at least made more time- and cost-effective.

Traditionally, the first therapy session or two is spent on intake, asking lots of questions to gather information about the client. I'd replace that by having the therapist, in advance of the session, email a probing questionnaire for the client to complete at home and email to the therapist a day before the session. Not only would that save the client time and money, it would give both client and therapist a chance to reflect on the questions rather than have to try to be maximally insightful on the spot.

I believe it's worth creating a video version of the new-client questionnaire. Of course, each therapist could create his or her own but I'm wondering if the following is worth a try: An eminent, eclectically oriented psychotherapist would create a probing new-client questionnaire, available on YouTube. I believe that many clients would prefer seeing that world-class therapist ask the questions and might give them greater thought.

More therapists should offer sessions by phone or SkypeVideo. I've found that, if the client is open to it, those are nearly as effective as in-person sessions. Not only does phone/Skype therapy avoid the client having to trek to and from the therapist's office, it gives clients more therapists from whom to choose. That's especially important for clients in locales with few top therapists, for example, rural areas.

Of course, every situation is different, and in severe cases, longer-term therapy may be needed but I believe that, in many cases, psychotherapy need consist only of one two-hour solution-generation session followed by one one-hour session to assess how helpful the solution(s) have been and, if needed, to tweak solution(s) and/or generate new ones.

How could it all be done in two sessions? Not only is there the efficiency that comes from a probing new-client questionnaire reviewed by the therapist in advance, the therapist and client knowing there's only one session to develop solutions motivates them to make the most of the session time. (Remember Parkinson's Law: Work expands to fill the time allotted?) Too often, much time in therapy sessions is wasted on unimportant tangents. Another benefit of developing the solution(s) in one session is that both therapist and client have all the input currently in-mind rather than having to recall it from notes and memory of the previous session(s.)

If possible, therapists should try to elicit solutions from the client--they're more likely to be helpful and to be acted upon. But unlike in traditional models of therapy, sometimes the client really does need and is open to the therapist's input. So if a therapist would like to suggest a possible solution, s/he should do so. The key, however, is to offer input in a client-empowering way, for example, "Would you mind if I suggest something?" With assent, then say something like, "I'm not sure I'm right but I'm wondering if it might help if you did (*insert strategy*.) What do you think?"

Other time-effective techniques used in psychotherapy and coaching should be part of the therapist's repertoire. One example: Ask the client, "If I waved a magic wand and your problem were solved, how would your behavior be different?" After they explain, ask, "Could you change any of that now?"

Unlike in many traditional therapy sessions, the first session should end with a specific behavior(s) that the client is enthusiastic about trying. Examples:

- The moment an irrational fear enters consciousness, say "Stop" and ask yourself, "What's the next positive step I can take?"

- Be aware of the moment of truth, for example, the moment you're about to start eating.

- Write a letter of reconciliation to your mother. Set it aside for a day. If it still feels good, send it.

- Every time you start a meal, say aloud, with expression, "I deserve to be good to myself and that means eating fewer calories." That will build the brain memory neurons associated with that constructive thought.

In the follow-up session, the client should report the extent to which the solution(s) have been helpful. If changes are needed, the therapist should, as recommended above, usually first try to get solutions to come from the client. If the client didn't do the homework, the therapist should try to ascertain if that was because of a fear, ran into a problem, the assignment ended up feeling inappropriate, etc., and try to help ensure that, subsequently, the client be more likely to complete that or a more appropriate assignment.

At the end of the second session, unless it's clear that more sessions are needed, it's often best to end with something like, "I think you now have the tools you need. So do you agree we don't need to see each other for a while?" If the client agrees, the therapist should say something like, " I do care about you and so I'd welcome your emailing me about your progress, if you have a quick question, feel free to ask, and if you do feel you need another session, just let me know." That makes the client feel supported, assures the client that s/he can have more sessions, and increases the chances that therapists get feedback that can improve their effectiveness.

More attention should be paid to the new iPhone/Android apps that provide app-based tools for anxiety, PTSD, etc., for example, T2 Mood Tracker[163] and Mobylize[164].

To comment, click HERE[165].

REINVENTIONS OF SPIRITUALITY

37
RELIGION REINVENTED

Religion can offer much that's good: a sense of community, a chance to do good for others, opportunities for socialization, a sense of morality, and hope for a better life, on earth or in heaven.

Alas, religion has a dark side: Priests sexually abuse children and their supervisors cover it up. Televangelists and deathbed-visiting clerics bilk elders out of their life savings with promises of salvation. Terrorists blow up buildings and airplanes so Allah can give them virgins in heaven.

And then there are religion's less-obvious liabilities:

Churches teach that "God will provide" and so people fail to take action to improve their lives.

People give money to churches that is often misspent and that would do more good elsewhere.

People look at others who don't practice their religion as lesser human beings, when religiosity, let alone church attendance, is a poor indicator of one's character.

Religion discourages logical thinking, emphasizing faith. Perhaps America's religiosity is one reason we form so many beliefs irrationally.

My personal belief is that there is no God worth praying to. After all, would a loving God allow billions of people to die in natural disasters and of terrible diseases? Why would God make some people born homosexual if homosexuality is a sin? Why would God say "Thou shall not kill" and then say "Kill all infidels? If "God will provide," why does more than half the world's seven billion people lack basic food, shelter, and health care?

Secular spirituality

Yet a *secular* spirituality informs nearly everything I do:

- As I supervise my assistant, I feel an almost sacred responsibility to make her worklife as rewarding as possible--After all, she's giving me some of the best hours of her life.

- As I decide what projects and clients to take on and what to write about, I feel a secular spiritual obligation to choose the things that would make the biggest difference to the world.

- As I decide what to buy, I remember that, even though my individual contribution is trivial, it's cosmically right to live lightly on the earth, to leave it better than when I entered it.

- That I have a secular spiritual obligation to enrich the lives of everyone I meet, from the Comcast repairman to the Trader Joe's cashier, to my wife. With her, that often includes staying out of her way so she can fully flower and enjoy, although it also includes giving unwanted advice when I feel the benefits of doing so outweigh the liabilities.

  A client asked me, "How is spiritual atheism different from trying to make the world better?" The reason I do the things I do go a step beyond "trying to make the world better." My core motivation is more universal--a cosmic responsibility to make the biggest possible impact during the time I am alive. I strive toward such goals simply because that seems the most worthy way to live life.

One liability of spiritual atheism: I rarely have what I call "Christian glow"-- those Christians who walk around wearing a beatific smile. Spiritual atheism usually doesn't make me feel good. It just feels like the right way to live, an obligation.

Judaism reinvented

Because I grew up in the Jewish tradition, I have special thoughts about reinventing Judaism:

The Jewish religion is dying:

- More than half of Jews intermarry.
- 2/3 of those intermarried couples raise their children not-Jewish.
- Anti-Israel sentiment and fear of anti-Semitism are deterring ever more Jews from self-identifying as Jewish.
- Jewish religious services are incompatible with most modern Jews' desires. Typically, services are two to three hours long, much in

114

Hebrew. Not surprisingly, most Jews today, in both the U.S. and Israel, are non-observant, except perhaps attending Rosh Hashanah and/or Yom Kippur services and/or attending a Passover seder.

- Most Jews are agnostic or, like me, atheist: not interested in praying to an "almighty God" who would allow earthquakes that kill thousands, Holocausts that kill millions, and horrifically painful cancers that kill billions, including infants.

The (ahem) savior for Jews: convert Judaism from a religion to a cultural affinity group, what I call *Secular Judaism*. Most Jews, if they're honest, often prefer the company of other Jews, just as other cultural, racial, and ethnic groups often prefer people from similar backgrounds. People may publicly claim to celebrate diversity but look at their choices of friends and it's clear that birds of a feather often flock together.

Most Jews, for example, like that Jews, *on average*, are intelligent, expressive, and committed to making a difference, whether in science, non-profits, business, or the arts. Most Jews' spiritual needs get largely or completely met through secular humanism.

So I believe the traditional hub of Jewish life, the synagogue, needs to be replaced with secular alternatives, for example, Jewish community centers such as the one in San Francisco[166] and informal meeting places such as those that can be created and managed online at MeetUp.com.

Tools like Facebook and Twitter can create live and virtual secular Jewish events and conversations. I also think that entities such as JDate.com could broaden their mission from dating to friends to Chavurah[167] (a sort of substitute family) to mentor/protégé matching.

Most groups need leaders but I believe the traditional Jewish leader, the rabbi, need be replaced by secular leaders, for example, the de facto leaders that would emerge from a regularly meeting group, or someone who took the initiative to start a group on meetup.com.

Another concept I believe is worth exploring is a hybrid religious/secular Sabbath service. Even many secular Jews enjoy listening to or singing a few familiar prayers. The problem is that a service is two hours of prayers, many in Hebrew plus many repetitions of praise to "Almighty God."

I was a guest Rabbi and created a service consisting of a few of the most familiar, nostalgia-inducing prayers, thought-provoking sections of the prayer book, and a discussion of why they came to synagogue that night. If asked to do it again, I might pick a topic of particular interest to Jews such as Israel/Palestine, intermarriage, or even a secular Tikkun Olam (heal the earth) topic such as capitalism versus socialism.

To comment, click HERE[168].

38
THE PASSOVER SEDER REINVENTED

I have been thinking about how a Passover Seder might become a more meaningful experience.

As an atheist, I'm not comfortable having a religious service praising the power of God, especially a God that could have imposed the horrific Ten Plagues on anyone. Even if we view the Exodus story as allegorical, an ode to freedom, I believe there are better triggers for an exploration of freedom's complexities.

Also, I believe the Haggadah (the booklet listing the Seder's ordained prayers, rituals and retelling of the Jews' flight from slavery in Egypt) is, net, an impediment to the Seder's meaningfulness.

As a result, the Seder I led last Passover consisted of the following:

1. The day before the Seder, I emailed the attendees this *Huffington Post* article, The Biblical Exodus Story is Fiction[169].

2. We lit candles to create a special atmosphere.

3. We made a toast to our making this the most rewarding Seder possible.

4. I asked each of the six attendees, "If this were to be the most rewarding Seder imaginable for you, what would you hope to get from it?"

5. I asked each participant to lead the group in their favorite part of the seder: a particular song, hiding or seeking the afikomen, the haroseth, the mortar/haroseth sandwich, the 10 drops of wine representing the Ten Plagues, the four cups of wine, etc. The key rituals and elements of the Exodus story emerged from the participants' choices.

6. I asked each attendee to say or perform something inspirational. Examples:

- A personal anecdote, perhaps related to Passover's freedom theme.
- Something inspiring about Israel.
- An aphorism that inspires the person.
- A song

I paced things so the Seder took one hour.

Perhaps the attendees were a biased sample or were simply being polite but all said it was quite a meaningful seder.

Whatever religious traditions you follow, might you want to reinvent one of yours? Would America be better if we looked afresh at our religious traditions?

To comment, click HERE.

39
TOWARD A MORE
ETHICAL SOCIETY

Most people know the right thing to do. The challenge is getting them to do it.

In just one week in my private practice, clients, in the confidentiality of my office, said the following:

- "Lawyers often double-bill."

- "I'm going to stay on unemployment until the extensions run out. Then I'll look for a job. Meanwhile, I'm working under-the-table."

- "I want to milk the education thing as long as I can so I don't have to grow up." (Professional students waste class slots that could have gone to people who would use that slot to be productive, to better society.)

- "I flirt to get what I want from my boss and then to gain power, I claim I feel violated when they flirt back."

- A physician admitted to me that some doctors do procedures, including surgeries, that could have more wisely been treated with drugs. Why? Simply to make more money.

All that on top of the corporate excesses, priests having sex with parishioners (including children,) people lying on the resumes and income taxes, using another person's urine to pass drug tests, hiring people to write their theses, etc., etc., etc.

Of course, getting people to more often do the right thing would bring enormous benefits to society: from more honestly on tax returns to more circumspect decision-making to more honorable relationships, business and personal. If we were all more ethical, we'd have to spend less time, money, and resources policing: for example, the mountain of regulations that business must comply with, which nonetheless often don't foil those who wish to be unethical.

The question is, "How do we get more people to choose integrity over expediency?" Nearly every school, including business schools, teach ethics yet too often when it's expedient, people cut corners, sometimes big corners-- Enron and LIBOR come to mind. But lack of integrity is pervasive: from test cheating to resume cheating, from tax cheating to customer cheating--So often do salespeople withhold negative information about a product. And of course, the financial crisis started with people who couldn't afford to buy a home being told they could get a "stated-income" mortgage. So they signed up figuring that if their home declined in value they could simply walk away, leaving the bank to pay their loss. Then sleazy bankers and insurance companies packaged the mortgages in a way that would hide the bad loans. And the lack of integrity spiraled from there.

There will never be a perfectly ethical society but I believe the following will take us closer: **We must all come to believe that integrity must trump expediency.** Not for fear of punishment because there are too many times that lack of integrity won't get punished. We must believe that integrity trumps expediency *because it is cosmically right:* that our worth as a human being is centrally dependent on being a person of integrity.

Getting America more ethical

How do we get people to believe that, indeed believe it so strongly that they'll much more often choose integrity over expediency?

To effect such a fundamental change in people's values requires efforts than begin pre-school and continue well into adulthood:

Parenting education (as part of Lamaze and other pre-birth parenting education--e.g.,. in the post-birth hospital room), should stress the primacy of teaching your child that ethics must trump expediency. Parents need, through their actions more than their words, to make clear the primacy of integrity. For example, every time a parent takes their 12-year-old to a restaurant where kids *under* 12 eat free and the parent says, "My child is 12" and pays, the child gets the message that integrity indeed does trump expediency.

Pre-K-through-graduate school, every year or two, students should create (for example, as a term paper) a model ethics training program for slightly younger students. Such an approach immerses the students in the process, will cause less resistance than would a lecture, and provides an ongoing source of improved ethics courses. There need be only three rules for that course development:

- Its goal must be to change the fabric of a student's thinking process so s/he will almost reflexively choose ethics over expediency.

- It must be critical-incident based, e.g., for elementary school students: bullying, for high school students: cheating, for business-school students: withholding negative information to sell a product.

- It must put students in the shoes of the victim of the unethical behavior. For example, when, to make more money, a surgeon recommends surgery when drug treatment would do, imagine how the patient feels on hearing he "needs" surgery, how his family feels, how he feels when he's checking into the hospital, wheeled into surgery, and when he suffers post-operatively.

To extend the ethics curriculum beyond the school years, producers of public-service announcements, TV dramas and sitcoms, movies and video games should be encouraged to create story lines that present thorny ethical dilemmas: for example, where expediency would yield great benefit and the ethical violation to derive that benefit is not great.

I would be dishonest to say that I have always chosen integrity over expediency but my batting average is pretty good. And if, from childhood, that concept had been drummed into me as powerfully as the message that that working hard is important, perhaps I would even more often make the cosmically ethical choice.

To comment, click HERE[170].

CONCLUSION
From ideas to implementation to improvement

My guess is that if you've read this far, your reaction is: "Lots of good ideas but can they be implemented?"

You can implement some of the ideas yourself: in choosing a career, becoming successfully self-employed, getting more education, getting motivated, investing, parenting, finding a romantic partner, becoming more ethical, reinventing your religious traditions, etc.

But with regard to this book's macro ideas, I share your concern about implementability. I'm far from the first person to propose bold ideas for creating a better society. And indeed most of them died without being substantially implemented. As I said in the introduction, that's a price of democracy: requiring broad buy-in leads to very slow, incremental changes.

I find some hope in that the Internet's wide availability enables good ideas to spread worldwide very quickly, to use the current argot: to go viral.

My hope, of course, is that some of these ideas do go viral. If you find yourself excited about one or more of this book's ideas, you might spread the word: Copy and paste it onto your website or blog. Tweet a link to it. Post a YouTube video. Start a thread on an online discussion group. Or go low-tech and chat with a friend about it or convene a salon/Town Hall meeting at your home. At the risk of cliché, the journey of 1,000 miles begins with a single step. I hope you take one.

In any event, I do hope that your reading this book was stimulating, perhaps of your own ideas for improving our world or your sphere of influence within it. At minimum, I hope it was a rewarding couple of hours.

Thank you for reading and for thinking.

To comment on the book as a whole, click HERE.

Marty Nemko

ENDNOTES
(Links spelled out for readers of this book's printed edition)

[1] http://s3.documentcloud.org/documents/213045/nytcbspoll.pdf

[2] http://i2.cdn.turner.com/cnn/2011/images/06/08/june.8.pdf

[3] http://static.businessinsider.com/image/4e0c8a2bcadcbbe570110000-590/democrats-tend-to-think-the-future-looks-good.jpg

[4] http://www.visitshanghaicity.com/2011/01/in-pisa-test-top-scores-from-shanghai-stun-experts.html

[5] http://dyson.cornell.edu/faculty_sites/gb78/wp/JLE_6301.pdf

[6] http://www.ici.org/viewpoints/view_11_reid_active_passive

[7] http://mutualfunds.about.com/od/Index-Investing/a/Why-Index-Funds-Beat-Actively-Managed-Funds.htm

[8] http://www2.ed.gov/about/overview/fed/10facts/edlite-chart.html

[9] http://www.usgovernmentspending.com/education_spending

[10] http://en.wikipedia.org/wiki/Achievement_gap_in_the_United_States

[11] http://en.wikipedia.org/wiki/Marva_Collins

[12] http://www.usatoday.com/news/education/2011-03-28-1Aschooltesting28_CV_N.htm

[13] http://www.schoolsmatter.info/2010/06/new-kipp-study-flawed.html

[14] http://www.khanacademy.org/#algebra

[15] http://edreach.us/2011/03/15/khan-academy-great-idea-with-one-glaring-hole/

[16] http://martynemko.blogspot.com/2012/05/reinventing-how-we-think.html

[17] http://www.cbo.gov/publication/22008

[18] http:/martynemko.blogspot.com/2011/02/reinvented-election-system.html

[19] http://womenshistory.about.com/od/quotes/a/camille_paglia.htm

[20]http://assets.theatlantic.com/static/front/images/magazine/covers/210x280/201007.jpg

[21] http://creativity-online.com/work/jc-penney-beware-of-the-doghouse/14501

[22] http://3.bp.blogspot.com/-REGjzKeq_LY/T53intthiXI/AAAAAAAARXw/PHTklVvROe8/s1600/degrees1.jpg

[23] http://www.bls.gov/news.release/empsit.t02.htm

[24] http://www.bls.gov/iif/oshwc/cfoi/cfch0009.pdf

[25] http://www.fas.org/sgp/crs/natsec/RS22452.pdf

[26] http://www.warrenfarrell.com/articles.php?id=12

[27]
http://online.wsj.com/article/SB10001424052702303592404577361883019414296.html

[28] http://www.compensationcafe.com/2012/02/3-years-after-ledbetter-still-talking-about-the-wrong-metric.html

[29] http://www.city-journal.org/2011/21_3_gender-gap.html

[30] http://www.sba.gov/about-sba-services/7367/5524

[31] http://www.infoplease.com/ipa/A0005148.html

[32] http://en.wikiquote.org/wiki/Madeleine_Albright.

[33] http://www.soroptimist.org/

[34] http://www.washingtonpost.com/opinions/cdc-study-on-sexual-violence-in-the-us-overstates-the-problem/2012/01/25/gIQAHRKPWQ_story.html?sub=AR

[35] http://www.afsp.org/index.cfm?page_id=04ECB949-C3D9-5FFA-DA9C65C381BAAEC0

[36] http://www.pnas.org/content/early/2011/02/02/1014871108.abstract

[37] http://www.cdc.gov/nchs/data/nvsr/nvsr59/nvsr59_09.pdf

[38] http://www.google.com/imgres?hl=en&safe=off&client=firefox-a&hs=nYs&rls=org.mozilla:en-US:official&biw=2144&bih=1007&tbm=isch&tbnid=0emM4eMBAaq-oM:&imgrefurl=http://skreened.com/girlsofgaming/girls-rule-boys-drool&docid=0QKVzb8TfbKHbM&imgurl=http://skreene

[39] http://www.whitehouse.gov/administration/eop/cwg

[40] http://whitehouseboysmen.org/blog/

[41] http://www.whitehouse.gov/blog/2012/04/06/white-house-forum-women-and-economy

[42] http://martynemko.blogspot.com/2010/06/beginning-of-men.html

[43] http://www.health-care-reform.net/causedeath.htm

[44] http://martynemko.blogspot.com/2010/11/nemkocare-how-id-do-health-care-reform.html

[45] http://www.avaresearch.com/ava-main-website/files/20100401061256.pdf?page=files/20100401061256.pdf

[46] http://www.acponline.org/clinical_information/journals_publications/ecp/novdec00/sox.htm

[47] http://www.medpac.gov/documents/jun09_entirereport.pdf

[48] http://en.wikipedia.org/wiki/Multiple_mini_interview

[49] http://www.amsa.org/amsa/homepage/takeaction/amsaoncall/12-01-18/Medical_Education_Reform.aspx

[50] http://martynemko.blogspot.com/2011/08/national-defense-reinvented.html

[51] http://martynemko.blogspot.com/2011/08/reinventing-our-justice-system.html

[52] http://www.economist.com/node/21534799

[53] http://ntu.org/tax-basics/who-pays-income-taxes.html

[54] "New Estimates of the Compliance Cost of Income Taxation," Committee on

Ways and Means, Subcommittee on Oversight, Hearing on Tax Simplification, invited written testimony given June 15, 2004.

55

http://online.wsj.com/article/SB10001424052748704116404576262761032853554.html

[56] http://www.bizjournals.com/pittsburgh/print-edition/2012/01/13/tax-gap-reaches-450b-unreported-income.html

[57] http://finance.yahoo.com/news/thousands-federal-workers-owe-back-taxes-231332510.html

[58] http://taxes.about.com/od/statetaxes/a/City-Income-Taxes.htm

[59] http://www.atr.org/files/files/VAT%20Hidden%20Costs.pdf

[60] http://www.bls.gov/ooh/Business-and-Financial/Accountants-and-auditors.htm#outlook

[61] http://ssa-custhelp.ssa.gov/app/answers/detail/a_id/240/~/2012-social-security-tax-rate-and-maximum-taxable-earnings

[62] http://martynemko.blogspot.com/2011/02/how-id-reinvent-taxation.html

[63] https://personal.vanguard.com/us/funds/byobjective/detail?category=TEBondLT

[64] https://personal.vanguard.com/us/funds/vanguard/onefund

65

https://personal.vanguard.com/us/funds/snapshot?FundId=0102&FundIntExt=INT

[66] https://personal.vanguard.com/us/FundsSnapshot?FundId=0103&FundIntExt=INT

[67] http://martynemko.blogspot.com/2011/08/reinventing-investing.html

[68] http://www.modulartoday.com/

[69] http://www.quietrock.com/

[70] http://www.acousticalsource.com/floor-soundproofing.html

[71] http://www.citiquiet.com/

[72] http://martynemko.blogspot.com/2011/08/housing-reinvented.html

[73] http://articles.latimes.com/2012/apr/04/business/la-fi-tn-flying-car-pal-v-test-flight-20120403

[74] http://en.wikipedia.org/wiki/Ignition_interlock_device

[75] http://www.beacongraphics.com/brightbike.htmlhttp:/goo.gl/hzu6Q

[76] http://en.wikipedia.org/wiki/Corporate_Average_Fuel_Economy

[77] http://martynemko.blogspot.com/2011/08/transportation-reinvented.html

[78] http://martynemko.blogspot.com/2011/08/reinventing-public-library.html

[79] http://israel21c.org/technology/innovation/made-in-israel-the-top-64-innovations-developed-in-israel/

[80] http://www.jewishvirtuallibrary.org/jsource/Judaism/nobels.html

[81] http://martynemko.blogspot.com/2010/03/new-israel-solution-to-palestinian.html

[82] http://online.wsj.com/article/SB10001424053111904537404576554750502443800.html?mod=googlenews_wsj

[83] http://www-eaps.mit.edu/faculty/lindzen.htm

[84] http://www.marshall.org/experts.php?id=44

[85] http://www.nytimes.com/2009/03/29/magazine/29Dyson-t.html?_r=2

[86] http://nipccreport.org/

[87] http://martynemko.blogspot.com/2011/06/reinventions-climate-change.html

[88] http://ntu.org/tax-basics/who-pays-income-taxes.html

[89] http://martynemko.blogspot.com/2012/04/contribution-points-economy-first-draft.html

[90] http://martynemko.blogspot.com/2011/09/why-obamas-jobs-plan-wont-workand-what.html

[91] http://www.nytimes.com/2009/07/06/us/06retrain.html

[92] http://www.insidehighered.com/news/2011/01/18/study_finds_large_numbers_of_college_students_don_t_learn_much

[93] https://www.google.com/finance?client=ob&q=INDEXDJX:SUNIDX

[94] http://books.google.com/books?id=CmVCSceuFRkC&dq=%22What+got+us+here+won%27t+get+us+there%22+goldsmith

[95] http://martynemko.blogspot.com/2011/09/why-obamas-jobs-plan-wont-workand-what.html

[96] http://www.dol.gov/elaws/elg/

[97] http://www.xcelhr.com/blog/Home/entryid/52/The-Facts-about-Employment-Lawsuits.aspx

[98] http://www.dol.gov/dol/topic/workcomp/index.htm

[99] http://hr.blr.com/whitepapers/Benefits-Leave/FMLA-Leave-of-Absence/12-Ways-to-Curb-FMLA-Abuse/

[100] http://www.hup.harvard.edu/catalog.php?isbn=9780674025721http://www.hup.harvard.edu/catalog.php?isbn=9780674025721

[101] http://www.bloomberg.com/news/2011-10-25/ford-quality-slumps-as-japanese-dominate-consumer-reports-automotive-ranks.html

[102] http://www.cato.org/publications/commentary/big-threes-shameful-secret

[103] http://www.bailoutcost.com/

[104] http://media.americanpetproducts.org/press.php?include=138687

[105] http://media.americanpetproducts.org/press.php?include=138687

[106] http://www.geekdesk.com/default.asp?contentID=628

[107] http://www.geekdesk.com/

[108] http://www.eeoc.gov/facts/ada18.html

[109] http://celiacdisease.about.com/od/sociallifestyleresources/f/Does-The-Americans-With-Disabilities-Act-Cover-People-With-Celiac-Disease.htm

[110] http://chronicfatigue.about.com/od/copingatwork/a/ADA.htm

[111] http://www.eeoc.gov/policy/docs/psych.html

[112] http://g3ict.org/resource_center/CRPD_Progress_Report_On_ICT_Accessibility_2010

[113] http://blog.pacificlegal.org/2012/obama-administration-taking-disparate-impact-theory-to-a-new-level/

[114] http://martynemko.blogspot.com/2012/05/if-youre-employed-youre-probably-asked.html

[115] http://martynemko.blogspot.com/2011/04/while-i-am-critical-of-many-aspects-of.html

[116] http://martynemko.blogspot.com/2009/01/dont-do-what-you-love.html

[117] http://martynemko.blogspot.com/2008/09/one-week-job-search.html

[118] http://martynemko.blogspot.com/2012/02/definitive-guide-to-replacing.html

[119] http://martynemko.blogspot.com/2010/07/career-counseling-reinvented.html

[120] http://en.wikipedia.org/wiki/Richard_Posner

[121] http://martynemko.blogspot.com/2011/05/toward-life-well-led-meter.html

[122] http://www.visitshanghaicity.com/2011/01/in-pisa-test-top-scores-from-shanghai-stun-experts.html

[123]
http://www.acf.hhs.gov/programs/opre/hs/impact_study/reports/impact_study/executive_summary_final.pdf

[124] http://cty.jhu.edu/summer/about/index.html

[125] This was data cited to me by Clifford Adelman, senior researcher at the U.S. Office of Education. Published statistics are aggregated across all students and for no longer than six years. Here is an example: www.higheredinfo.org/dbrowser/?level=nation&mode=graph&state=0&submeasur

e=27

[126] http://en.wikipedia.org/wiki/Vocational_education

[127] http://martynemko.blogspot.com/2011/04/education-americas-most-overrated.html

[128] http://martynemko.blogspot.com/2010/06/blueprint-for-reinventing-education.html

[129] http://www.knewton.com/flipped-classroom/

[130] http://martynemko.blogspot.com/2012/05/dream-team-taught-courses-breakthrough.html

[131] http://www.acf.hhs.gov/programs/opre/hs/impact_study/reports/impact_study/executive_summary_final.pdf

[132] www.thenationalcampaign.org/resources/pdf/pubs/WhatWorks.pdfhttp:/www.thenationalcampaign.org/resources/programs.aspxhttp:/www.thenationalcampaign.org/resources/pdf/pubs/whatworks09.pdf

[133] http://archive.k4health.org/toolkits/implants/implanon

[134] http://en.wikipedia.org/wiki/Acting_white

[135] http://phys.org/news159626393.html

[136] http://www.theatlantic.com/business/archive/2012/04/53-of-recent-college-grads-are-jobless-or-underemployed-how/256237/#

[137] http://www.urbandebate.org/urbandebateworks2.shtml

[138] http://martynemko.blogspot.com/2011/08/my-plan-for-closing-achievement-gap.html

[139] http://martynemko.blogspot.com/search/label/higher%20education%20critique

[140] http://www.insidehighered.com/news/2011/01/18/study_finds_large_numbers_of_college_students_don_t_learn_much

[141] http://en.wikipedia.org/wiki/Collegiate_Learning_Assessment

[142] http://martynemko.blogspot.com/2011/07/college-report-card-making-colleges.html

[143] http://chronicle.com/article/50K-Club-of-College-%20Prices/129527/

[144] http://martynemko.blogspot.com/2012/04/college-campus-needs-to-go-extinct.html

[145] http://chronicle.com/article/50K-Club-of-College-%20Prices/129527/

[146] http://martynemko.blogspot.com/2010/10/utopia-u-my-blueprint-for-model.html

[147] http://thehill.com/polls/173173-the-hill-poll-most-voters-see-media-as-biased-unethical-and-cozy

[148] http://www.gallup.com/poll/1654/honesty-ethics-professions.aspx

[149] http://newsroom.ucla.edu/portal/ucla/Media-Bias-Is-Real-Finds-UCLA-6664.aspx

[150] http://learning.blogs.nytimes.com/2011/08/29/test-yourself-math-aug-29-2011/

[151]
http://www.republican.senate.gov/public/index.cfm/files/serve?File_id=8602a3e0-1f9e-4f39-9226-87597cdf4da4http://message.snopes.com/showthread.php?t=78562

[152] http://www.nationalreview.com/campaign-spot/271107/white-house-nuh-uh-stimulus-jobs-only-cost-185k-each#

[153] http://martynemko.blogspot.com/2012/05/worried-warriors-musings-on-media-bias.html

[154]
http://www.people.vcu.edu/~mamcdani/Publications/McDaniel_Whetzel_Schmidt_Maurer%20%281994%29.pdf

[155] http://www.criteriacorp.com/resources/employers.php

[156]
http://professionals.collegeboard.com/profdownload/Validity_of_the_SAT_for_Predicting_First_Year_College_Grade_Point_Average.pdf

[157] http://martynemko.blogspot.com/2011/08/whom-to-pick-reinventing-

selection.html

[158] http://www.scientificamerican.com/article.cfm?id=parents-peers-children

[159] http://www.divorcerate.org/

[160] http://www.independent.co.uk/environment/overpopulation-is-main-threat-to-planet-521925.html

[161] http://martynemko.blogspot.com/2008/09/family-is-overrated.html

[162] http://martynemko.blogspot.com/2012/01/need-relationship-help-try-couples.html

[163] http://t2health.org/apps/t2-mood-tracker

[164] http://www.preventivemedicine.northwestern.edu/behavioralmedicine/Mohr%20Lab/mohrlab.htm?study_name=mobilyze#project

[165] http://martynemko.blogspot.com/2011/08/psychotherapy-reinvented.html

[166] https://www.jccsf.org

[167] http://en.wikipedia.org/wiki/Chavurah

[168] http://martynemko.blogspot.com/2011/01/replacement-for-judaism.html

[169] http://www.huffingtonpost.com/staks-rosch/the-biblical-exodus-story-is-fiction_b_1408123.html

[170] http://martynemko.blogspot.com/2010/11/ethics-education-most-important-topic.html

Made in the USA
San Bernardino, CA
20 August 2016